THE REDISCOVERY OF TEACHING

"Internationally renowned as a philosopher of education, Biesta as 'educator' turns to teaching in the fourth volume in his study of contemporary education, in this age of control through learning. In life and work, Biesta is the epitome of a commitment to the formation of student and teacher *subject-ness*, his evolved central concept. The result for both can be new possibilities in and with the world. Surely such a vision is sorely needed today."
—*Lynda Stone, Samuel M. Holton Distinguished Professor,*
The University of North Carolina at Chapel Hill, USA

"This is the most politically engaging of Biesta's four books on emancipatory education. He challenges us to give teaching back to education. He does this by exploring existentially what it means to be a teacher and what it means to exist as a teacher. While being philosophical, Biesta uses very accessible language and includes various practical implications. I thoroughly recommend this book for all those who care about education."
—*Scott Webster, Senior Lecturer in Education, Deakin University, Australia*

"In this groundbreaking work, Gert Biesta refreshingly reminds us what every small child in school instinctively knows—that teachers make or break the educational experience. Biesta vividly demonstrates, with nuance and philosophical craft, the unique and irreplaceable work that teachers do. Arguing against too much measurement, and indeed against too much learning, this work is an inspiring reminder that teaching is not primarily about control but rather about emancipation."
—*Charles Bingham, Professor, Faculty of Education,*
Simon Fraser University, Canada

"The 'fourth volume' of Gert Biesta's highly acclaimed educational trilogy is a signpost for the post-neoliberal era in education. It elaborates and elucidates the complex argument for teaching that cannot be replaced by learning, or explained in constructivist terms. With provocative examples, Biesta illustrates the transition from the egotic immanence of learning to ethical teaching that interrupts the ease of comprehension. In fact, Biesta speaks of teaching that is close to every teacher's experience: unpredictable, challenging, and performed with empty hands, with no instruments of certainty. But rather than denouncing it as not fit for the new world, he deeply re-theorizes it and gives it a critical, political edge."
—*Tomasz Szkudlarek, Head of the Department of Philosophy of Education and*
Cultural Studies, Institute of Education, University of Gdansk, Poland

THE REDISCOVERY OF TEACHING

Gert J. J. Biesta

Routledge
Taylor & Francis Group

NEW YORK AND LONDON

First published 2017
by Routledge
711 Third Avenue, New York, NY 10017

and by Routledge
2 Park Square, Milton Park, Abingdon, Oxon OX14 4RN

Routledge is an imprint of the Taylor & Francis Group, an informa business

© 2017 Taylor & Francis

British Library Cataloguing in Publication Data
A catalogue record for this book is available from the British Library

Library of Congress Cataloging in Publication Data
A catalog record for this book has been requested

ISBN: 978-1-138-67069-3 (hbk)
ISBN: 978-1-138-67070-9 (pbk)
ISBN: 978-1-315-61749-7 (ebk)

Typeset in Bembo
by Taylor & Francis Books

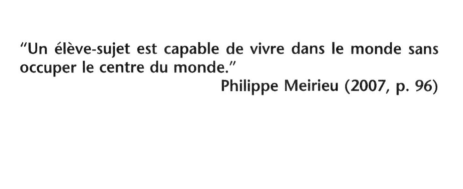

"Un élève-sujet est capable de vivre dans le monde sans occuper le centre du monde."

Philippe Meirieu (2007, p. 96)

CONTENTS

ACKNOWLEDGEMENTS

This book is the fourth monograph in what I have previously described as a trilogy, consisting of *Beyond Learning* (2006), *Good Education in an Age of Measurement* (2010), and *The Beautiful Risk of Education* (2014). Just as there was some risk in referring to that set of books as a trilogy – suggesting a sense of completion – there is also some risk, and a little irony, in adding a fourth title to the collection. The main question here is whether I have anything new to say in addition to what I have already said in my writings so far. This judgement is, of course, entirely for the reader to make. The only thing I can say in my defence is that I felt that my critique of the language of learning (*Beyond Learning*), of the impact of the global measurement industry on education (*Good Education in an Age of Measurement*), and of the desire to make education entirely risk-free (*The Beautiful Risk of Education*) needed to be complemented by a robust and explicit account of the importance of teaching and the teacher.

There are significant *intellectual* reasons for this, which I outline in the chapters that follow, just as there are important *educational* reasons for it, which I discuss extensively as well. But surrounding all this are important *political* reasons for making the case for teaching and the teacher. This is particularly so given developments in contemporary educational policy that seem to have lost an interest in teachers and their teaching. This claim may sound remarkable in light of the many policy documents that keep repeating that the teacher is the most influential factor in the educational process. Yet what I find problematic about this claim, and in a sense even objectionable, is the reduction of the teacher to the status of a *factor*, that is, to a variable that shows up in the analysis of data about the educational production of the small set of measurable learning outcomes that apparently "count". In my view this is not a case for the importance of teaching and teachers at all, but amounts more to an insult – something that many teachers, who are nowadays subjected to a way of thinking that makes their salary, their career, and their livelihood dependent upon the extent to which they have been able to perform as such a "factor", will probably attest (see Carusi in press).

For quite some time I have toiled with the idea of giving this book the subtitle "progressive arguments for a conservative idea". The reason for this has to do with the fact that the case for teaching and the teacher not only needs to be made in response to the reduction of the teacher to a factor, but also in response to trends towards the "learnification" (Biesta 2010a) of education; trends that see the teacher as a facilitator of learning rather than as someone who has something to bring to the educational situation and who has something to give to students, even if what is on offer is just a quick question or a brief moment of hesitation (Biesta 2012a). For those who see the turn towards learning predominantly as a turn away from teaching-as-control, any argument in favour of teaching and the teacher can probably only be perceived as a conservative move. Much of what I will try to put forward in the chapters that follow is to argue that teaching is not necessarily conservative and not necessarily a limitation of the child's or the student's freedom, just as the "freedom to learn" (Rogers 1969) is not automatically or necessarily liberating and progressive.

Over the years I have been heartened by the positive responses to my work, particularly from those who find the questions I raise and the language I use to pursue those questions helpful for articulating in a more precise manner what matters in their own educational endeavours. Although I cannot deny that my work is to a large extent of a theoretical nature, I do not think that this means that it is without significance for educational practice. This is not just because I am convinced that language really matters for education, but also because I believe that the best way to counter attempts at simplifying and controlling the work of the teacher is by making the practice and practising of education itself more *thoughtful*. This requires that we keep trying to think differently about education in order to see how such thinking might make a difference in the everyday practice of education. The ideas offered in this book are therefore not just meant as ideas to think *about* – and hence to agree or disagree with – but perhaps first and foremost as ideas to think *with*.

Although I am solely responsible for the content of this book, the ideas put forward are the fruit of many interactions, conversations, discussions, moments of insight, things I have been taught, and teachings I have received. Chapter 1 has its origin in the work I have been doing for a significant number of years now with colleagues at NLA University College in Bergen, Norway. Their focus on "pedagogikk" and their concern for the existential dimensions of education and life continue to provide a nourishing environment for exploring what really matters in education. I particularly would like to thank Paul Otto Brunstad, Solveig Reindal, and Herner Saeverot for their work on the edited collection in which a first version of the ideas presented in chapter 1 appeared. And I would like to thank Tone Saevi for her generous work in translating my ideas into Norwegian. An earlier version of chapter 2 was written to mark the end of my tenure as editor-in-chief of *Studies in Philosophy and Education*. I have thoroughly enjoyed serving the international philosophy of education community in this role, although it has been hard work. The journal is now in the capable hands of Barbara Thayer-Bacon. I would also like to express my thanks to the students who took part in the course I discuss in chapter 2. I am grateful for what they gave me and am grateful for what was given to us.

An earlier version of chapter 3 was written in response to an invitation from Guoping Zhao. I would like to thank her for the opportunity and for the insightful questions she keeps asking about my work. I would also like to thank Vanessa de Oliveira and Wouter Pols for the many conversations that have shaped my thinking on the topics of this chapter. Alex Guilherme provided me with an opportunity for developing my ideas about the role of the teacher in emancipatory education, on which I report in chapter 4. My thinking on this topic has also benefited greatly from the work I did with Barbara Stengel for the *AERA Handbook of Research on Teaching*. Chapter 5 has its roots in my long-standing collaboration with Carl-Anders Säfström, particularly the work we did on the *Manifesto for Education* (Biesta & Säfström 2011). I am grateful for the many generative conversations we have had over the years. They engage with serious issues, but are always also good fun. I would also like to thank Herner Saeverot and Glenn-Egil Torgersen for introducing me to the theme of the unforeseen in education. Joop Berding's work on Janusz Korczack remains an important source of inspiration.

I see academic work as work, and although it is very privileged work, it is not all there is in life. I am grateful to my wife for reminding me about this, and for everything she has taught me about education. I would like to thank Brunel University London for giving me a job at a difficult time in my life and career, and the colleagues in the Department of Education for making me feel at home. The original trilogy was published by Paradigm Publishers, USA, and I remain very grateful to Dean Birkenkamp for the encouragement and support over the years. I would also like to thank Catherine Bernard at Routledge for her confidence in the current project, and for her patience.

Perhaps two "health warnings". First of all, this is not a perfect book. This is not just because I think that perfection is a dangerous ambition, but also because the way I am searching for the progressive meaning of teaching remains that: a search that is still ongoing. I hope, nonetheless, that where and how I am searching makes a useful contribution to the discussion. Secondly, I am aware that in places what is to follow is highly theoretical and philosophical. I encourage the reader to stay with those passages, even if they do not immediately reveal their meaning, as they are important layers of what I seek to explore in this book as well.

Finally: although I do not envisage adding a fifth title to the trilogy, one can of course never be sure about what the future will bring. In my view, however, a quartet is also not a bad achievement.

Edinburgh, December 2016

PROLOGUE: THE NEED FOR A RE(DIS)COVERY OF TEACHING

"I enjoy surprising my students by telling them that I am a conservative, that I have striven throughout my life to 'conserve our radical tradition.'"

George Counts (1971, p. 164)

The point I seek to make in this book is that teaching matters. In itself this may not be a very contentious claim, and in certain circles it has actually become quite popular to argue that the teacher is the most important "factor" in the educational process (see e.g. OECD 2005; McKinsey & Co. 2007; Donaldson 2010; Department for Education 2010), albeit that we should be wary of referring to the teacher as a mere factor. The real issue, however, is not *whether* teaching matters; the real issue is *how* teaching matters and what teaching matters *for*. It is in relation to these questions that the discussion already becomes a bit more complicated, because in recent years the role and position of teaching and the teacher have been challenged from two different but in a sense complementary angles.

One development concerns the impact of the rise of the language and the "logic" of learning on education, a development that has shifted the attention away from teaching and the teacher towards students and their learning (see Biesta 2006, 2010a). The rise of the language and logic of learning has transformed the teacher from a "sage on the stage" to a "guide on the side" – a facilitator of learning, as the expression goes – and even, according to some, to a "peer at the rear". While the idea of the teacher as a fellow learner or of the classroom as a community of learners may sound attractive and progressive, such learning-centred depictions of education tend to provide rather unhelpful and in my view ultimately misleading accounts of what teaching is, what the work of the teacher is, and what students might gain from encounters with teaching and teachers. The ideas put forward in this book are therefore an attempt at the *recovery* of teaching in an age of learning, and at the *rediscovery* of the significance and importance of teaching and the teacher.

Yet making a case for the importance of teaching and the teacher is not entirely without problems. A major difficulty stems from the fact that in recent years the suggestion that teaching matters has been made most vociferously from the more conservative end of the spectrum, where teaching is basically approached in terms of *control* and where the control of the work of the teacher itself has also emerged as a major issue (see Priestley, Biesta & Robinson 2015; Kneyber & Evers 2015). One version of this argument is the idea that the best and most effective teachers are those who are able to steer the educational process towards the secure production of a small set of pre-defined "learning outcomes" and a limited number of pre-specified identities, such as those of the good citizen or the flexible lifelong learner. There is not only an ongoing research effort focused on generating evidence about what apparently "works" in relation to this ambition (see Smeyers & Depaepe 2006; Biesta 2007). There is also a "global education measurement industry" (Biesta 2015) eager to indicate which systems perform best in producing the desired outcomes. The call for education as control and for teachers as agents of control is also voiced through concerns about an apparent loss of authority in contemporary society and the suggestion that education is the key instrument for restoring such authority, including the authority of the teacher itself (see, for example, Meirieu 2007). What is often (conveniently) forgotten in such discussions is that authority is fundamentally a *relational* matter (see Bingham 2008) and not something that one person can simply impose onto another person.

The main problem with the idea of teaching as control, with the depiction of teaching as an act of control, and with the suggestion that teaching ought to be a matter of control, is that in such configurations students can only appear as *objects* of the teacher's intentions and actions, but not as *subjects* in their own right. This has been the main bone of contention in all the criticisms of authoritarian forms of education, culminating in calls for the abolishment of the very "project" of education altogether, such as in the case of the anti-education movement (*Anti-pädagogik*) which emerged in Germany in the late 1960s (see von Braunmühl 1975). What is interesting, and in a sense remarkable, is that the teacher has been a recurring target of this critique. The assumption here seems to be that teaching can ultimately only be understood as something that *limits* the freedom of students and thus hinders the possibility for them to exist as subjects in their own right.[1] This is a major reason why attempts at (literally) dethroning and side-lining the teacher ("from the sage on the stage to the guide on the side") and at refocusing education on students, their learning, their sense-making, and their active construction of knowledge – to name some of the main trends in contemporary educational thought and practice – are generally seen as liberating and progressive moves.

In such a context and climate it seems that any attempt at making a case for the importance of teaching and the teacher can only be perceived as a step backwards, as a conservative rather than a progressive contribution to the discussion. It is important to see, however, that this only follows if we conceive of what it means to exist as subject in terms of what Hannah Arendt has aptly characterised as the idea of *freedom as sovereignty* (Arendt 1977[1961], pp. 163–165), where to be free, to exist as free subject, means *not* to be influenced by anything or anyone outside of oneself. The question, however, is whether this is a viable conception of what it means to exist as subject.[2] One major line in the chapters that are to follow seeks to argue that this is *not* the case, and that to exist as subject actually means to be in an ongoing "state of dialogue"[3] with what and who is other – a "state of dialogue", moreover, where our subject-ness is not constituted from the inside out, that is, from our intentions and desires, but is intimately bound up with the ways in which we engage with and respond to what and who is other, with what and who speaks to us, addresses us, calls us, and thus calls us forth.

When we begin to think about our existence as subject along these lines, teaching starts to gain a new significance, first and foremost because as an "address" that comes to us from the outside – we might also say: an address that transcends us (see Biesta 2013a) – it is no longer automatically limiting or even obstructing the possibility for us to exist as subject, but may well be the very "event" that opens up possibilities for us to exist *as subject*. This is indeed the other major line in the chapters that are to follow, where I will explore teaching in its significance for subject-ness, its significance for our existing *as subjects*. Here, as I will suggest, teaching becomes concerned with opening up existential possibilities for students, that is, possibilities in and through which students can explore what it might mean to exist as subject in and with the world. Along these lines teaching begins to appear as the very *opposite* of control, the very opposite of attempts at approaching students merely as objects, but rather takes the form of approaching students as subjects even, as I will argue, when there is no evidence that they are capable of it.

There are three reasons why I believe that the ideas explored in this book may matter. The first has to do with the fact that in the domain of education teaching has generally become positioned at the conservative end of the spectrum, while most of what opposes teaching – such as the focus on student learning, on their meaning-making and knowledge construction, on their creativity and expression – is seen as liberating and progressive and as supporting and enhancing subject-ness. We find this represented, for example, in the ongoing "swing" from curriculum-centred to child-centred and student-centred conceptions of education. What is remarkably absent in the discussion is the consideration of a *third option*, one where teaching is positioned at the progressive end of the spectrum and is (re)connected with the emancipatory ambitions of education. What I seek to offer in this book is such a third option – a set of progressive arguments for what is nowadays generally seen as a conservative idea. My ambition is not only to rediscover the progressive significance of teaching, but also to show that a focus on student learning, on sense-making, construction, creativity, and expression – ideas that are often presented as ways to counter education as control – may in itself have little to do with enhancing the possibilities for students to exist as subject.

To exist as subject, as I will suggest, means being in a "state of dialogue" with what and who is other; it means being exposed to what and who is other, being addressed by what and who is other, being taught by what and who is other, and pondering what this means for our own existence and for the desires we have about our existence. To exist as subject therefore means that we engage with the question of whether what we desire is desirable, not only for our own lives, but also for the lives we try to live with others on a planet that has limited capacity for fulfilling all the desires projected onto it. Such a way of understanding what it means to exist as subject stands in some tension with what many see as a major tenet of our times, where our freedom as human subject is predominantly understood as the freedom of *choice*: the freedom to choose what we want to choose, to do what we want to do, to have what we want to have, to be what we want to be, and also buy what we want to buy. The approach towards human subject-ness that is pursued in this book therefore also raises some wider questions about this major trend in contemporary society – a society that Paul Roberts has characterised, very accurately in my view, as an "impulse society" (Roberts 2014).

A third reason why the ideas put forward in this book may be of importance is in relation to more philosophical discussions about human being and human beings. Whereas my ambitions with this book are not philosophical but educational, it may nonetheless be interesting to ponder one main philosophical implication from the arguments that are to follow, in which I seek to suggest that our human subject-ness may not be located in our capacity to learn, to make sense, to give meaning, and so forth, but is first and foremost to be found in our "ability"[4] to be addressed, to be spoken to, to be taught. This suggests, in its shortest formula, that the human being is not an animal who can learn, but rather a being who can be taught and can receive (a) teaching.

The book is organised in the following way. In chapter 1, *What Is the Educational Task?*, I ask the question what education is *for* and, more specifically, what there is for teachers, as educators, to do. The answer I propose is that the task of the educator is to make the grown-up existence of another human being possible or, with a more precise formulation: it is about arousing the desire in another human being for wanting to exist in the world in a grown-up way. I discuss what it means to focus education on the question of existence, what it means to exist in the world, and what it means to exist there in a grown-up way. I offer an understanding of grown-up-ness that doesn't see it as the outcome of a developmental or educational trajectory but rather as a way of existing in and with the world, a way where the question of whether what we desire is what we should be desiring has become a living question, a question we carry with us and bring into play in every situation we encounter. I discuss what a focus on this question requires from the teacher and explore the implications for our understanding of the role of authority in education.

If the rediscovery of teaching is at least in part a response to the impact of the language and logic of learning in education, then a key question is how we should understand the relationship between teaching and learning. In chapter 2, *Freeing Teaching from Learning*, I suggest that learning is only one of the existential possibilities we have as human beings, and that teaching, if it is aimed at the grown-up subject-ness of the student, should actually endeavour to open up other possibilities for students to exist in and with the world – other, that is, than in terms of learning. In addition to an exploration of the literature on the relationships between teaching and learning, I discuss a course I taught in which I asked students to refrain from learning, that is, to refrain from sense-making and understanding. The course not only showed that education can indeed proceed meaningfully without learning, but also revealed that when we bracket learning, when we bracket our desire for understanding, the world can begin to speak to us, can begin to address us, can begin to teach us.

In chapter 3, *The Rediscovery of Teaching*, I continue the main line from chapter 2 by asking whether interpretation and sense-making are indeed central to the way in which we are in and with the world. The chapter is built around a close reading of insights from the work of Emmanuel Levinas, particularly with regard to the theme of sense-making or, in his terms, signification. Against the idea that human beings are basically "meaning-making animals" (my phrase) – a notion I explore in more detail through a discussion of the robot vacuum cleaner as a paradigm case of an intelligent adaptive system – Levinas puts forward the view that sense-making does not come *before* our encounter with the other but actually only arises *as a result of* the encounter with the other or, to be even more precise: as a result of the "experience" of being addressed by another (human) being. In the chapter I not only provide a discussion of the detail of Levinas's argument. I also pay explicit attention to the connection Levinas makes with the themes of subject-ness and freedom, showing how his thinking provides an argument against the idea that human freedom should be understood as the "freedom of signification". Levinas hints at a more "difficult freedom", which he describes as the freedom to do what only I can do.

If chapter 3 begins to build the argument why our grown-up existence as subject in and with the world is precisely *not* a matter of our sovereignty, *not* a matter of our freedom of signification, then we can begin to see that education aimed at the freedom of the student, education aimed at emancipation, is not to be understood as education that tries to keep all influences away from the student. This provides a way into the question of the role of the teacher in emancipatory education, which is the theme of chapter 4, called *Don't Be Fooled by Ignorant Schoolmasters*. In the chapter I compare three different conceptions of emancipatory education: neo-Marxist critical pedagogy, the work of Paulo Freire, and the ideas put forward by Jacques Rancière in his book *The Ignorant Schoolmaster*. I show how both Freire and Rancière respond to the potentially authoritarian dimensions of critical pedagogy. But whereas Freire locates this problem in the teacher,

Rancière locates it in the role of knowledge. Unlike Freire, therefore, Rancière is able to show why teachers and teaching remain important in emancipatory education.

In chapter 5, *Asking the Impossible: Teaching as Dissensus*, I explore what this means for the work of the teacher and, more specifically, for our understanding of the *act* of teaching. Against the idea that teaching aimed at the subject-ness of the student is a matter of "building up" – of helping the student to acquire the knowledge, skills, and dispositions that will make it possible for them to be a subject; teaching as a matter of empowerment – I explore a different route where, after Rancière, teaching operates as *dissensus*. Dissensus is not the absence of consensus but is about the introduction of an "incommensurable element" into an existing state of affairs. It is, to put it briefly, about approaching the student *as subject*, even – or particularly – when all the available evidence about what the student is capable of points in the opposite direction. Negatively, teaching as dissensus is enacted as a refusal to accept any claim to incompetence, particularly if such a claim comes from the student; positively, teaching as dissensus is enacted as an appeal to a future way of existing of the student, a way of existing that is yet unforeseen, both from the perspective of the educator and from the perspective of the student. But it is this very appeal, this very reference to the "impossible" as that which cannot be *foreseen* as a possibility (Derrida), that opens up a space where the student might appear as subject. I argue that anything less than this, any education that only wishes to proceed on the basis of what is possible, of what is visible, for which we have evidence, actually runs the risk of blocking this very future.

I conclude with a brief epilogue in which I summarise the main insights from the book and argue that teaching, if it is interested in the grown-up subject-ness of students, is not a matter of creating spaces where students can be free – that is, enact their freedom of signification, their freedom to learn – but is rather about creating existential possibilities through which students can encounter their freedom, can encounter the "call" to exist in the world in a grown-up way, as subject.

Notes

1 In chapter 4 I discuss how this has played a role in emancipatory conceptions of education, including Paulo Freire's work.
2 As I will explain in detail in the chapters to follow, I approach the question of human subject-ness in an existential way, that is, as a question about a way or modality of existing – hence the formulation "exist as subject".
3 The expression "state of dialogue" may sound a bit odd at this point as dialogue is rather seen as something dynamic and evolving rather than as a "state". The reason for this formulation is to highlight that dialogue is not to be understood as conversation but as an existential "form" – I return to this later.
4 "Ability" is put in quotation marks because being addressed, being spoken to, being taught are phenomena that cannot be generated by us but come to us from the outside, which means that we have little control over this "ability".

1

WHAT IS THE EDUCATIONAL TASK?

In this chapter I explore a simple and in a sense very basic question, which I have phrased as the question "What is the educational task?" I am aware that the phrasing of this question is not ideal, particularly not where it concerns the word "task". In a number of Germanic languages there are much more precise and much more interesting words to denote what I am after. In German there are the words "Aufgabe" and "Auftrag", which are very close to the Dutch words "opgave" and "opdracht". What these words try to hint at are things that need to be done, that are there for us to do when we find ourselves in a certain situation or position, such as the position of being a teacher or educator. This is less about a task that needs to be performed or a job that needs to be done, than it is about a responsibility we encounter. Interestingly, the words "Gabe" and "gave" actually mean gift, so that "Aufgabe" and "opgave" refer to a task *given* to us, a task that comes with the job, so to speak, or the responsibility that comes with the position. "Auftrag" and "opdracht" have the words "tragen" and "dragen" in them, which mean to carry – and that is what the task given to us is asking from us as well. That we carry this task. What I seek to express through the question of the educational task, therefore, is that education is not just anything we want it to be, but it comes with a particular "Aufgabe", a particular responsibility, a particular imperative, we might even say.

The answer I will suggest in this chapter is that the educational task consists in making the grown-up existence of another human being in and with the world possible. Or, with an even more precise formulation: the educational task consists in arousing the desire in another human being for wanting to exist in and with the world in a grown-up way, that is *as subject*. There are at least two aspects to this answer that need further exploration. One is the idea of "grown-up-ness", and the other the use of the word "existence". To begin with the latter: to use the word existence means that I wish to focus on the ways in which human beings exist, that is, in short, on *how* they are, and not on the question of *who* they are. If the latter is the question of *identity*, the former is the question of *subjectivity* or, in slightly more accurate terms: it is the question of human *subject-ness* or of the human "condition" of *being-subject*. Both questions – the question of *who* I am and the question of *how* I am – are of course legitimate questions, also in the context of education. But they are very different questions and it is important not to conflate them, neither at the level of concepts – the concepts of "identity" and "subject-ness" are not interchangeable – nor at the level of what these concepts seek to express.

As I will discuss in more detail below, I approach "grown-up-ness" – admittedly a slightly awkward word – not as a developmental stage or the outcome of a developmental trajectory, but in existential terms, that is, as a particular "quality" or way of existing. What distinguishes a grown-up way of existing from a non-grown-up way is that the grown-up way acknowledges the alterity and integrity of what and who is other, whereas in the non-grown-up way this is not "on the radar". The grown-up way acknowledges, in other words, that the world "out there" is indeed "out there", and is neither a world of our own making nor a world that is just at our disposal, that is, a world with which we can do whatever we want or fancy. "The world" here refers both to the natural and to the social world, both to the world of things and to the world of beings. It refers, more concretely, both to our planet and everything on it, and to the other human beings we encounter on this planet. It refers, with an interesting word proposed by Alfonso Lingis (1994, p. 123), both to the earth and to the "earthlings" inhabiting the earth. To acknowledge the alterity and integrity of this world is not to be understood as an act of generosity on my side to let what and who is other exist. It is, in other words, not my decision to let the world exist or not. It rather is my decision to give the alterity and integrity of the world a place in my life – or not, of course.

What is the justification for suggesting that the educational task is to make the grown-up existence of another human being in and with the world possible? In an absolute sense there is no justification for this and in this regard the suggestion is literally groundless. Yet this does not preclude that this suggestion may be meaningful, particularly when compared to alternative views about what the educational task might be. One point to highlight here is that it is actually only in the world that we can really exist, since when we withdraw ourselves from the world we end up existing only with and for ourselves – which is a rather poor and self-absorbed way of existing, if it is to exist at all. To exist in and with the world thus always raises the question of the *relationship* between my existence and the existence of the world. And here again, at least as a starting point, we can say that to exist in and with the world without making space for what exists there *as well*, is not really to exist in the world. The challenge, therefore, is to exist in the world without considering oneself as the centre, origin, or ground of the world – which is exactly how Philippe Meirieu describes the "student subject" ("élève-sujet"), namely as the one who is able to live *in* the world, without occupying the centre of the world[1] (see Meirieu 2007, p. 96).

But perhaps the even more difficult question is why we should think of this as an *educational* issue, rather than as something that each of us should figure out in our own lives. Why, in other words, should we even consider the suggestion that it would be the task – and hence the responsibility and perhaps even the duty – of one human being to make the grown-up existence of another human being possible? We could respond to this question by referring to the fact that this seems to be what educators have always been doing, that it is key to what it means to be a parent and that it is key to what it means to be a teacher, and that what I am trying to do is simply to explore what this might mean in our times. We could also say that the ambition to make the grown-up existence of another human being possible expresses an interest in freedom and, more specifically, an interest in the freedom of the *other*, and that this is key to what education ought to be about (see Biesta & Säfström 2011, p. 540). I do think that this is how we might *articulate* the educational interest and hence the educational task, but I do not think that this automatically amounts to a *justification* of it. After all, the promise of liberation has too often turned into another exercise of power (see, for example, Spivak 1988; see also Biesta 2010b and, for a wider discussion, Andreotti 2011), which means that in these matters we should proceed carefully and with not too many pretensions.

I will present my reflections on the educational task in five relatively brief steps, partly in connection to some ideas I have presented in more detail in earlier publications, and partly highlighting with more precision notions of "existence" and "grown-up-ness". I will first look at the notion of subjectivity or subject-ness and will try to articulate what it means to exist *as subject*. I will pursue this a little further by arguing next that existential matters are ultimately first-person matters rather than matters of theory. I will explain this distinction and indicate what this means for the question of being-subject and more specifically the idea of uniqueness. From here I will turn to the question of what it means to exist *in the world* – a question I will seek to answer by highlighting what it means *not* to be in the world. This will allow me to say a bit more about the distinction between grown-up and non-grown-up ways of being in the world and the importance of the distinction between the desired and the desirable. In the fifth and final step I reflect on the educational "work" that might contribute to making the grown-up existence of another human being in and with the world possible. I conclude the chapter with a brief reflection on the role of power and authority in educational relationships and on what this means for teaching and the teacher.

The Subject Is Subject

Given that I have suggested that what we are talking about is the subject-ness of the human being and not its identity, the first question to ask is what it means to be a subject. We can answer this question in two ways, either by looking at the subject itself and then trying to find out what the subject *is*, or by looking away from the subject and then asking what it means for the subject to *exist*. Here I pursue the second option, taking inspiration from Sartre's dictum that "existence precedes essence", that is, that we first of all exist, that we "find" ourselves in existence, and that any answer to the question of who we are comes afterwards.[2] While attempts to answer the question of what the subject is are not necessarily meaningless, they come, in a sense, always too late in relation to our existence itself. This means that while they may help to clarify dimensions of the human condition, they are not able to ground it. If, taking inspiration from Heidegger, we take the idea of existence in a literal sense, we can already begin to see one aspect of the existence of the subject, namely that to exist as subject does not mean to be with oneself – to be identical with oneself – but rather to be "outside" of oneself, that is, in some way to "stand out" ("ek-sist") towards the world and be "thrown" into it.

The main insight I wish to highlight about the existence *of* the subject and our existence *as* subject is that, to a large degree, our subject-ness is not in our own hands, which may even mean that it is not in our hands at all. The author whom I have found most helpful in making sense of this aspect of our subject-ness is Hannah Arendt, particularly her ideas on action (which, in Arendt's work, is a technical term with a very precise definition). Action – which for Arendt is one of the three modalities of the active life, the *vita activa* (Arendt 1958) – first of all means to take initiative, that is, to begin something. Unlike many philosophers who emphasise the mortality of the human being, Arendt looks in the opposite direction, that is, towards the capacity of the human to be a beginning and a beginner. Arendt compares action to the fact of birth, since with each birth something "uniquely new" comes into the world (Arendt 1958, p. 178). But it is not just at the moment of birth that this happens. Through our "words and deeds" we continuously bring new beginnings into the world.

Beginning is, however, only half of what action is about, because whether our beginnings will be of any consequence, whether our beginnings will "come into the world" (see Biesta 2006), depends *entirely* on whether and how *others* will take up our beginnings – and "taking up" needs to be understood in the broadest possible sense, so as to include responding to such beginnings, repeating such beginnings, taking such beginnings as a cue for further initiatives, and so on. This is why Arendt writes that the "agent" is not an author or a producer, but a subject in the twofold sense of the word, namely as the one who began an action and the one who suffers from and is literally sub-jected to its consequences (see Arendt 1958, p. 184). The upshot of this is that our "capacity" for action – which in this sense is precisely not a capacity we have or possess – crucially depends on the ways in which others take up our beginnings. In this sense we can say that our subject-ness is not in our own hands, which we might indeed summarise, as Simon Critchley (1999, p. 63) has done, by saying that "the subject *is* subject".

Although the uptake by others of our initiatives frustrates our beginnings, Arendt emphasises again and again that the "impossibility to remain unique masters of what [we] do" is the very condition and the *only* condition under which our beginnings can become real, that is, can come into the world (see Arendt 1958, p. 244). It is therefore also the only condition under which *we* can come into the world, that is, can exist as subjects. While it might be tempting to want to control the ways in which others take up our beginnings, the problem is that as soon as we do so we begin to deprive others of their opportunities for action, their opportunities to begin and to exist as subjects. We would then be after a world where *one* person can act – can be a subject – and everyone else is just a follower – and hence an object of the one who is subject. Arendt concludes therefore that action is never possible in isolation – which also means that we can never exist as subject in isolation. Arendt goes even as far as to argue that "to be isolated is to be deprived of the capacity to act" (p. 188). This, in turn, leads her to the simple but profound statement that "Plurality is the condition of human action" (p. 8), that is, that it is only under the condition of plurality that action for all – and hence subject-ness for all – is possible. It is important not to read this as an empirical statement, but rather as the normative "core" of Arendt's work, which is explicitly committed to a world in which everyone has the opportunity to act and exist as subject (see also Biesta 2010d).

Uniqueness as Irreplaceability

While Arendt helps us to give meaning to the idea that our subject-ness is not in our hands but to a large degree dependent on what others do with our initiatives, there are still two limitations to her approach – limitations that in a sense are connected. One limitation is that Arendt provides us with a *theory* about human subject-ness, and thus approaches the question of subject-ness from what we might call a *third-person perspective*. While her insights are illuminating, they nonetheless try to give a description of the condition of being-subject from the "outside", so to speak, rather than from the point of view of the existence of the subject itself – which we might refer to as a *first-person perspective*. The second limitation is that Arendt provides a *general* account of the condition of human subject-ness rather than an account of each human subject in its uniqueness. To put it a bit crudely: while Arendt gets us closer to understanding what it means for subjects to exist, she does not provide us with an argument for why it might matter that each individual human subject exists. Perhaps these observations sound vague and strange when made in this abstract way. But they are precisely what is at stake in the way in which Emmanuel Levinas approaches the question of human subject-ness, in that he tries to give an "account" of subject-ness not in the form of a theory but from a first-person perspective. Here subject-ness appears as something *I* have to "figure out", that no one else can figure out for me, and that I cannot figure out for anyone else. And the key term in Levinas's account is "uniqueness".

But uniqueness is a tricky term, as the first inclination we might have is to understand it from a third-person perspective, that is, as the question concerning the characteristics and capacities each of us has that make each of us different from everyone else. This we might refer to as the idea of *uniqueness-as-difference*, which would bring us immediately back to questions of identity and identification and to a perspective on uniqueness from the outside – where, from an abstract point, we can make clear how each human being is in some respect different from every other human being. As I read his work, Levinas hints at the need for asking a different question about uniqueness, which is not the question "What *makes* me unique?" – the question about what I have that makes me different from everyone else – but the question "*When does it matter* that I am I?" The latter question precisely does *not* ask about everything I have or possess that would distinguish me from others, but looks for situations, for existential events, where my uniqueness is "at stake" and where *I* am therefore at stake. The situations Levinas has in mind are those where someone calls upon me in such a way that the call is addressed at *me* and no one else. These are situations where the call comes to me, and where it is only *I* who can respond. They are, in other words, situations where we encounter a responsibility, which is the reason why Levinas suggests that responsibility is "the essential, primary and fundamental structure of subjectivity" (Levinas 1985, p. 95).

Alfonso Lingis (1994) provides the helpful example of a case where a friend who is dying asks to see you. Such a question, Lingis argues, is a question that only addresses *you*, as the friend is not interested in just seeing someone – she wants to see you and no one else. This is a question, therefore, that literally singles you out. It is a question that burdens you with a responsibility. It is for you to take up this responsibility or walk away from it. When Zygmunt Bauman summarises Levinas's insights by writing that for Levinas responsibility is "the first reality of the self" (Bauman 1993, p. 13), he captures what is going on here extremely well, as we could say that it is only in encounters where there is a responsibility for *me* that my uniqueness begins to matter, that my uniqueness is "at stake", that *I* am at stake. Here uniqueness is not a matter of difference – a third-person perspective – but a matter of *irreplaceability* – a first-person perspective. Uniqueness, as Levinas puts it, is about doing "what nobody else can do in my place" (Levinas 1989, p. 202). There is of course no one who can force us to take on the responsibility we encounter. In that regard it is important to see that Levinas is not describing this as a duty, as something we must do. Nor does he see it as a biological fact, that is, as something we cannot *not* do. On the contrary, we could say that in a rather strange sense human freedom also means that we have the possibility to walk away from the responsibility we find ourselves in – and this is entirely up to each of us individually. We cannot take on this responsibility for another human being, nor can we force another human being to act in a particular way if, that is, we respect their subject-ness, if, that is, we encounter them as subjects in their own right, and not as objects of our actions and intentions. (This has important implications for education, to which I will return below.)

A final thing to mention here is that the responsibility in relation to which my uniqueness begins to matter always and structurally comes from the outside rather than that it is generated by me. It does not start from a feeling or a need to be responsible for the other or to care for the other. The responsibility in the face of which my uniqueness begins to matter and in response to which I might realise, in that particular, singular moment, my subject-ness, therefore always appears as an interruption of my "immanence", an interruption of my being with and for myself. Levinas in some cases describes human subject-ness as "the very fracturing of immanence" (Levinas 1989, p. 204), or in slightly less "strong" language, as the moment where "the Same – drowsy in his identity" is *awakened* by the other (p. 209; emphasis in original).

Both Arendt and Levinas thus try to show how our subject-ness is not in our own hands. But whereas Arendt's account starts from my initiatives and is about how they need to be taken up by others in order to become real, Levinas puts this on its head by showing how the possibility for my subject-ness starts from the outside, and only *then* becomes an "issue" for me, and only and uniquely for me. And the "issue" is whether I respond to the responsibility I encounter and, in that moment, "realise" my subject-ness, or whether I walk away from it. If Arendt gives us a *theory* of the way in which our subject-ness is not in our own hands – and thus provides us with a third-person perspective – Levinas gives us something that is more like a *phenomenology* that engages with the question of subject-ness from a first-person perspective, by showing how subject-ness is ultimately a matter for each of us individually to figure out. While, as mentioned, theory might help, theory can never replace the existential question; theory can never replace the existential challenge and can sometimes actually become an excuse for not having to engage with it.

The Middle Ground between World-Destruction and Self-Destruction

If the previous two sections give us some insights into what it means to exist as subject, I now wish to shift to the second part of my thesis about the educational task, which is the suggestion that what matters educationally is to exist in and with the world in a grown-up way. Grown-up-ness, as I have already suggested, has to do with an acknowledgement of what I have referred to as the alterity and integrity of what and who is other. If this acknowledgement is not to be understood as generosity from my side – where I would "allow" the world to exist which, formulated in this way, actually sounds rather arrogant – then how might we make sense of what this means? One way to do this is through a discussion of what might happen when we – or in Arendtian language: our initiatives – encounter resistance.

The encounter with resistance, that is, the encounter with the fact that something or someone resists our initiatives, is a tremendously important experience as it shows that the world is not a construction of our mind or our desires, but actually has an existence and hence an integrity of its own. The experience of resistance is in that regard a worldly experience – an experience that we are *somewhere*, not just anywhere. What do we do, or what might we do, when we encounter resistance? Let me look at three possible options.

When our initiatives meet resistance, our first response might be one of irritation in the face of the encounter with something that frustrates or blocks our initiatives, or at least limits our ability to execute our initiatives. We might "blame" that which offers resistance for this, and might try to enforce our intentions – we could also say: enforce our will – upon that which offers resistance. This is partly what needs to be done in order for our initiatives to become real, to arrive in the world, but if we go too far in enforcing our will upon the world, we reach a point where our own force becomes so strong that it destroys the (integrity of the) very "entity" that offers resistance. If we think of our encounters with the material world, we may find ourselves pushing so hard that the material we want to shape and form breaks under the pressure. In this moment we end up destroying the very thing that offers resistance. We might say, therefore, that at this end of the spectrum of the encounter with resistance there is the risk of *world-destruction*.

From here we can begin to see what lies at the other end of this spectrum, because a second way to respond to the experience of resistance and, more specifically, to the frustration of this experience, is to withdraw from what offers resistance, to step away from it. This is where, when faced with the experience of resistance, we say that the situation is too complex and too difficult for us, that we don't have the energy or appetite to persevere, and we thus begin to withdraw ourselves from the encounter with what offers resistance – in plain English: we back off. While again there may be good reasons for doing so – as it leaves space for that which offers resistance to exist and be in the world – the risk here is that we ultimately withdraw ourselves from any engagement with the world, and ultimately withdraw ourselves completely from (existence in) the world. In a similar vein we could say, therefore, that we give up or destroy the very conditions that would allow us to exist in the world in the first place. Hence the extreme we find here is the risk of *self-destruction*.

World-destruction and self-destruction are the extreme responses to our encounter with resistance, our encounter with the world – responses where we actually end up outside of the world, in a place of *non-existence*. They therefore also mark the middle ground where existence – *worldly* existence, existence in and with the world – is possible and literally *takes place*. We might refer to this middle ground as *dialogue*, as long as we do not think of dialogue as conversation, but as an existential form, a way of being together that seeks to do justice to all partners involved. Dialogue is in this regard fundamentally different from a contest. A contest is an existential form aimed at bringing about winners and losers. Also, a contest comes to an end once someone has won, whereas dialogue is an ongoing, never-ending challenge. An ongoing, never-ending "Aufgabe", we might say. A contest requires a confined burst of energy; staying in dialogue requires ongoing and sustained energy, attention, and commitment.

The middle ground is not an easy place to be, which partly helps to understand the attraction of the extremes of world-destruction and self-destruction, as they provide escapes from the difficulty of existing in and with the world. Sometimes we do need to retreat from the difficult middle ground, perhaps to recharge our batteries or gain a perspective on what we are encountering there. And sometimes there is a need to "push" for something better, which also shows that the middle ground is not the space where just anything should exist. But it is ultimately *only* in the middle ground that existence is possible. The middle ground is therefore not a place of pure self-expression, but rather a place where our self-expression encounters limits, interruptions, responses – which all have the quality of the frustration Arendt talks about, and the fracturing of immanence Levinas refers to. But with Levinas we can also say that these experiences awaken us from our drowsy state of being outside of the world, of being just with ourselves. These experiences tell us that we are in it "for real" – where what I *do* matters, where how I *am* matters, and where *I* matter. To stay in the middle ground thus requires that we affirm and perhaps even embrace this difficulty as the very difficulty that makes our existence possible. Staying in the middle ground thus requires a desire for a worldly existence, an existence outside of ourselves – ek-sistence. And the educational task, as I have suggested, is to arouse such a desire in another human being.

"Grown-up"-ness, the Desired, and the Desirable

Given how I have described grown-up-ness in the beginning of this chapter, that is, not as the outcome of a developmental process but as an existential quality or quality of existing, it may perhaps not be too difficult to see that the middle ground between world-destruction and self-destruction is the place where a grown-up way of being with what and who is other might be achieved. By referring to grown-up-ness as something that might be *achieved* I am again highlighting the existential thrust of the line of thinking I am putting forward in this chapter. This means that grown-up-ness is not to be understood as something we can possess or claim to have. It is also not something we can claim to be, if by such a claim we would mean that it is securely in our possession and would permeate everything we do. Whether we manage to achieve a grown-up way of being with what and who is other, is something that is always at stake and always a question. In each new situation we may, after all, fail to engage in a grown-up way and while it is important that we keep making an effort – if, that is, we desire to exist rather than being with ourselves – we can never be certain of the outcome of our efforts, and can even be surprised (and disappointed) by our own actions and responses.

While grown-up-ness is not an ideal term, particularly not because of its reference to processes of growth and thus to the suggestion that grown-up-ness is the outcome of such a process – which I have argued that it is not – grown-up-ness does refer to a state where we have managed to overcome another way of acting with and responding to what and who is other, a way which I have characterised as non-grown-up, but which we could also call infantile (but see below), egocentric, or, with a term suggested by Levinas, egological,[3] that is, following the logic of the ego, not the logic of what and who is other. The egological way of being is entirely generated by the desires of the ego, without asking – and this is the crucial distinction – whether, how, or to what extent such desires are desirable, both for the ego's existence in and with the world and for the world in and with which the ego seeks to exist.

This means, and this is important, that grown-up-ness is not a suppression of desires, but a process through which our desires receive a reality check, so to speak, by asking the question of whether what we desire is desirable for our own lives and the lives we live with others. Such a question – and this is educationally important – always poses itself as an *interruption* of our desires. Such an interruption partly manifests itself through the experience of resistance, and we could even say that when we encounter resistance we not only encounter the world but at the very same time we encounter the desires we have in relation to the world.

When we encounter resistance we could say that the world is trying to tell us something – and perhaps we could even say that the world is trying to teach us something. But the interruption can also be actively enacted when someone asks us whether what we desire is actually desirable. And of course, we may also reach a situation where this question becomes our own question, where it becomes a living question in our own lives. (I return to the educational significance of this below.) In all this, therefore, the ambition is not to eradicate our desires, but to give them a worldly form and quality so that they can support and sustain a grown-up way of being in and with the world. Spivak (2004, p. 526) uses the interesting expression of an "uncoercive rearrangement of desires" and gives this as her definition of what education is and what it is about.

By using the opposition of "grown-up" and "infantile" in this existential way I am not trying to give children a bad name or assume that all adults are able to exist in a grown-up way. On the contrary, by understanding the infantile and the grown-up, the egological and the non-egological as two different ways in which we can engage with what and who is other, I aim to make visible that both options are open for children *and* for adults – and perhaps we should say that we can only ever know retrospectively whether we have turned out in a particular situation as child-like or adult-like. Our age and the size of our body are no secure indicators for that.

A final observation to make here is that while we do need to pay attention to what is there to do uniquely for each of us, we should not forget that the environments in which we act and live send out strong and influential messages as well. To the extent to which modern life is structured by the logic of capitalism, we could say that we live in an environment that is precisely *not* interested in interrupting and limiting our desires, but rather is focused on the multiplication of our desires, so that we will desire more and therefore will buy more and more. Such an "impulse society" (Roberts 2014) is precisely not interested in our grown-up-ness but rather prefers that we remain infantile, as that's where the money is being made.

The Educational Work: Interruption, Suspension, and Sustenance

If this has brought us sufficiently, albeit not perfectly close to an understanding of what it might mean to exist in and with the world in a grown-up way, that is *as subject*, I now wish to say a few things about the particular educational work[4] that might contribute to making such an existence possible.

Perhaps the most important point to make, particularly in response to fashionable ideas of education as having to do with the promotion of the child's development, with helping students to develop all their talents and reach their full potential, is that the main principle of education aimed at making a grown-up existence in and with the world possible is that of *interruption*. This line partly follows from Arendt's reflections on the condition of being subject – as they highlight that our subject-ness is not in our own hands. But it follows most explicitly from the line of thought pursued by Levinas and his suggestion that the event of my subject-ness always appears as an *interruption* of my immanence, the being for and with myself, and as an awakening out of this drowsy state.

Whereas Levinas's formulations may sound abstract, the main insight here is relatively simple if we see, for example, that we all have talents for good and for evil, and that both morality and criminality can be understood as outcomes of developmental processes. This immediately shows that the educational task can never just be the promotion of the child's development, but needs to be concerned with the question of which development is desirable and which is not – which means that the fundamental educational gesture is that of interrupting and questioning development. It also shows that the educational task can never just be about letting students develop all their talents and reach their full potential because, again, what we should be after is the interrogation of talents and potential in order to explore which talents are going to help and which talents are going to hinder grown-up ways of being in the world – which necessarily requires an interruption rather than just letting everything emerge, grow, flow, and flourish. To suggest that education is just about supporting the child's development, just about letting each student develop their talents and reach their full potential, is therefore an educational lie – a lie that is not only misleading towards children and students, but also misleading as a vocabulary for educators to describe their task and even understand what it actually is.

Whereas interruption is, in this regard, the most important term as it highlights the fundamental structure of the educational work, it is important to see that interruptions can be performed in a number of different ways – some of them educational (that is aimed at enhancing grown-up-ness) and some of them not. One uneducational way to enact interruption is in the form of what we might call *direct* moral education, where the interruption is enacted as a direct judgement on the side of the educator about the child and their beginnings, that is, in the form of condemnation – "Wrong!" – or praise – "Right!" The problem here is not the feedback in itself, which is important and to a certain degree useful, but the fact that the judgement comes from the educator and is applied *to* the child, as this gives the child no time and no opportunity to appear as subject in relation to such a judgement. The child remains no more than an object of the educator's judgement (or, for readers who can cope with a little play with words: the child remains subjected to the educator's judgement).

We can also put this in terms of the distinction between the desired and the desirable. This distinction, as I have suggested, marks the difference between an infantile and grown-up way of existing, but it is important to read this carefully, as the idea is not that "desires" are the infantile way and "desirable" the grown-up way. It is rather that the grown-up way is characterised by the "ability" – but perhaps we should call it a willingness or a desire itself – to make and ponder the distinction between one's desires and their possible desirability. The difference, in other words, is that between being an object of one's desires – or in a more precise formulation: being *subjected to* one's desires – and being *a subject of* one's desires.

As long as the educator decides for the child or student which of their desires are desirable, the child and student remain objects of the educator's intentions and activities. The key educational challenge, therefore, is not simply to tell the child or student which of their desires are desirable, but for this question to become a living question in the life of the child or student. This requires anything *but* direct moral education, but rather hints at the need for opening up literal and metaphorical spaces where the child or student can establish a relationship with their desires, just as it requires the creation of a gap between the desires as they arise and the actions that follow from them. The educational principle here is that of *suspension* – a suspension in time and space, so we might say – that provides opportunities for establishing relationships with our desires, to make them visible, perceivable, so that we can work on them.[5] This, to make the point one more time, is not a process in which we overcome or destroy our desires – our desires are, after all, a crucial driving force – but one in which we select and transform our desires so that we move from being subjected to our desires to becoming a subject of our desires. This is the "uncoercive rearrangement of desires" Spivak writes about (Spivak 2004, p. 526), which is perhaps a little less uncoercive than her formulation suggests and, in addition to rearrangement, may also involve a change in the intensity of our desires.

Interruption and suspension both take place in the middle ground with the ambition to keep the student in the middle ground, as it is only there that grown-up-ness can ever be achieved. This means that a third dimension of the educational work – and perhaps this is the most important and most precarious dimension – is that of supporting the student with staying in the difficult middle ground. It involves providing *sustenance*, in any imaginable form, so that the student can endure the difficulty of existing in and with the world. Yet, as the middle ground is the place where the student encounters the world, part of the educational work here is also to make this encounter possible and give it form – which has to do with pedagogy and curriculum. More specifically the task is to give form to the experience of resistance, so that there is a real possibility to experience the world in its alterity and integrity. It thus also means to provide time to encounter the experience of resistance and work with it – or, to use a useful and interesting expression: to work *through* it.

The work of the educator here is also to "stage" the experience of resistance as important, meaningful, and positive and to have an eye for the many different ways in which this can be done. This is not about making things difficult for the sake of making them difficult, but about acknowledging their crucial significance vis-à-vis the question of being in the world as subject. Viewed in this way it is a warning against taking all resistance out of education, by making it flexible, personalised, and completely tailored to the needs of the individual child or student. Such strategies run the risk of isolating the student from the world rather than supporting the student in engaging with the world. To show the student where and how the encounter with the experience of resistance is educationally meaningful – which is not just by telling them that this is so, but can take many different forms – is important in order to keep the child away from the two extremes of world-destruction and self-destruction. Or, in opposition to the "negative" language of "keeping away", the work of the educator is to arouse the desire in the student for wanting to stay in the difficult middle ground.

Transforming Power into Authority: The Beautiful Risk of Teaching

If interruption, suspension, and sustenance are, in a sense, rather concrete activities, there is one further dimension of the work of the teacher that is barely, if at all, in the hands of the teacher. This dimension has to do with the transformation of power into authority. The issue here is that although educational interruptions are "aimed" at the subject-ness of the student, when enacted they appear as acts of power, at least in those cases where students did not ask for such interruptions to occur – which is probably where all education starts. The ambition of educational interruptions is to "turn" students towards the question of whether what they desire is what they should be desiring, and much of the work of the educator is about creating time, space, and forms so that students can encounter their desires, examine their desires, select and transform them. Whereas the question of the desired and the desirable is introduced by the teacher – as a powerful interruption – the ambition is that this question becomes a living question in the life of the student. At stake here is the question as to what should have authority in our lives, and the question of authority is precisely about coming into dialogue with what and who is other. It is about letting something or someone have power in our lives. It is about authorising what and who is other, it is to let it speak, so to say, to make it into an author.

What we hope as teachers whose teaching is aimed at the subject-ness of our students is that at some point the student will turn back to us and acknowledge that what in the first instance appeared as an unwanted interruption – an act of power – did actually contribute to their grown-up existence in and with the world, their grown-up subject-ness. When such a turning happens, and only when it happens, we can say that power – which is always monological and one-directional – has transformed into authority – which is always dialogical and relational (Bingham 2008). But we never know *whether* such a "return" may happen, and we never know *when* such a "return" may happen, which may well be long after the student has disappeared from our view and our (professional) life. This means that any teaching aimed at the subject-ness of the student is first of all risky in that its outcomes are unpredictable. But it is also risky because we, as teachers, risk ourselves, as we are always enacting power without often knowing whether this power will "return" as authority, as accepted and acknowledged power. But this should not prevent us from taking this risk, because without it education would not happen either. It rather should help us to understand much better what the risky nature of teaching and education more generally is, if it is aimed at the subject-ness of the student, if it is aimed at arousing the desire in another human being for wanting to exist in the world in a grown-up way.

Concluding Comments

In this chapter I have tried to answer the question as to what the educational task – or perhaps we can now say, what the educational responsibility and the responsibility of the educator – is by suggesting what the educational work should aim for or be interested in: arousing the desire in another human being for wanting to exist in a grown-up way. I have tried to make clear what the focus on existence entails, highlighting the importance of existing in the difficult middle ground between world-destruction and self-destruction. I have also tried to give new meaning to the idea of grown-up-ness by seeing it in existential rather than developmental terms. And I have tried to indicate the particular work of the teacher, if teaching is aimed at the subject-ness of the student, highlighting the role of interruption, suspension, and sustenance. Through this I have begun to reconnect teaching with questions of emancipation and freedom, with the educational interest in the grown-up subject-ness of students. In the next chapter I explore what this means for the question of learning in education and, more specifically, for the relationship between teaching and learning.

Notes

1 In French: "Un élève-sujet est capable de vivre dans le monde sans occuper le centre du monde."
2 Sartre writes in *Existentialism Is a Humanism* (Sartre 2007[1946]) that "man first of all exists, encounters himself, surges up in the world – and defines himself afterwards" (p. 28).
3 In English translation the actual term Levinas uses is "egology" – see Levinas (1969[1961], p. 35).
4 I use the word "work" here in a very loose sense, with no particular theoretical pretensions.
5 In Biesta (2017) I discuss in much detail the particular contribution that the arts can make in this process.

2

FREEING TEACHING FROM LEARNING

If the task of the rediscovery of teaching is at least in part a response to the impact of the language and logic of learning on education, then a key question is how we should understand the relationship between teaching and learning. This is the question I explore in this chapter, arguing that learning is not necessarily what teaching is or ought to be about or is or ought to aim for. To free teaching from learning, as I will put it, may therefore open up new and different existential possibilities for students, particularly opportunities for encountering what it means to exist in and with the world in a grown-up way – opportunities that may be precluded if we tie teaching too closely to learning.

Driving a wedge between teaching and learning may, however, not be that easy because, at least in the English language, the phrase "teaching and learning" has become so ubiquitous that it often feels as if it is one word, *teachingandlearning*, and that the connection between teaching and learning is as tight and necessary as the phrase seems to suggest. But what actually is the relationship between teaching and learning? Does teaching necessarily lead to learning? Should the sole ambition of teaching be to promote or bring about learning? Can we assume that teaching causes learning? Is the relationship between teaching and learning therefore to be understood as a relationship of cause and effect? Or is it a relationship between the meaning of concepts, so that to use the word "teaching" without assuming the word "learning" makes no sense? Are "teaching" and "learning" necessarily connected? Is it possible to think of teaching outside of the confines of learning? Can teaching be meaningful if it explicitly tries to keep students away from learning? And for what reasons might that be a good idea?

I engage with these questions not only in order to clarify the relationship between teaching and learning, but also in order to explore some of the limits and limitations of the alleged connection between teaching and learning. This is important for theoretical reasons, because questions about the relationship between teaching and learning appear to go to the heart of educational practice. But it is also important for political reasons, as it can help to get a better sense of what teachers can be held responsible for and what not. This is particularly urgent given the fact that politicians and policymakers nowadays are often expecting far too much from teachers, particularly with regard to what, in unhelpful language, is referred to as the "production" of "learning outcomes".

I begin this chapter with a review of literature on the relationship between teaching and learning, particularly focusing on contributions from the theory and philosophy of education. The main aim of this step is to raise some questions about the suggestion that teaching and learning are necessarily and intimately connected. I then indicate some problems with the recent rise of the language of learning in educational research, policy, and practice, highlighting how the "learnification" (Biesta 2009a) of educational discourse has marginalised a number of key educational questions, particularly regarding the purposes of teaching and of education more widely. Against this background I zoom in on the idea of the learner, asking what, in common understandings of learning, it actually means to exist as a learner. Here I particularly focus on the idea that learning is to be understood as an act of sense-making or comprehension. After this I raise an epistemological and an existential question. The epistemological question has to do with the difference between knowing and meaning-making as processes of construction (literally sense-*making*) and as processes of reception. The existential question has to do with the difference between being in the world as a constructor, as a receiver, or as one being addressed or spoken to by who and what is other. Against this background I present, in a final step, a concrete example of a course I taught in which I asked my students to refrain from sense-making and understanding, that is, to refrain from learning.

The Teaching–Learning Connection: On Teaching, Studenting, and Pupilling

A helpful place to start the discussion is by asking whether the overall intention of teaching should be to bring about learning. While many would probably at first sight respond to this question with an "of course", there are a number of reasons why it might make sense to keep teaching and learning a bit more separate from each other. One obvious reason for doing so is to stay away from the mistaken idea that teaching can be understood as the *cause* of learning. This idea, which is connected to notions of teaching as an intervention, to learning as an outcome, and to mechanistic understandings of the complexities of education, is problematic because it puts the entire responsibility for the achievements of students on the shoulders of the teacher. It thus suggests that students are merely willing objects of intervention rather than thinking and acting subjects who carry responsibility for their part of the educational process. So what then is the relationship between teaching and learning? And what should teachers intend to bring about, if it is not learning?

With regard to the first question some authors have argued that the relationship between teaching and learning is not a relationship between *events* – which is the assumption underlying the idea that teaching is the cause of learning – but rather a relationship between *concepts*, so that the meaning of the word "learning" is included in the (proper use of the) word "teaching", or that the meaning of the word "teaching" is included in the (proper use of the) word "learning". The latter suggestion can easily be refuted, as it is obvious that people can learn without teaching (which doesn't preclude that there may be learning that actually requires teaching). Refuting the first suggestion is slightly more difficult, and there are indeed authors who have argued that the concept of "teaching" *necessarily* involves the concept of "learning". Here is, for example, how John Dewey put it:

> Teaching may be compared to selling commodities. No one can sell unless someone buys. We should ridicule a merchant who said that he had sold a great many goods although no one had bought any. But perhaps there are teachers who think they have done a good day's teaching irrespective of what people have learned. There is the same exact equation between teaching and learning that there is between selling and buying. (Dewey 1933, pp. 35–36)

While at a very general level Dewey's suggestion makes sense, we nonetheless need to be careful. This is not only in order to make sure that people do not read a statement about the relationship between *concepts* as a claim about an alleged relationship between *events*. (In the foregoing quote Dewey actually gets quite close to doing this himself.) It is also because, at a conceptual level, the word "teaching" can be used correctly without the need for the teaching to have resulted in learning. The latter has to do with some ambiguities in the word "teaching".

Paul Komisar (1968) has made a very helpful distinction between teaching as an *occupation*, as a general *enterprise*, and as an *act*. Occupation, enterprise, and act provide three different answers to the question as to what a person is doing when he or she says he or she is teaching. Saying this can first of all mean that the person either is a teacher (occupation) or is engaged in the activity of teaching. With regard to the latter Komisar has suggested a further distinction between the general "enterprise" of teaching and specific "acts" of teaching. Teachers spending an hour with their students may be engaged in the enterprise of teaching but not everything they do (e.g. handing out worksheets, lining up their students, showing a video-clip) may count as an act of teaching. Komisar gives the slightly more interesting example of a situation where a teacher has been expressing his own prejudices about a topic but then stops doing so "and is finally teaching again" (Komisar 1968, p. 174). This suggests that to identify a particular act as an instance of teaching is not a factual matter but actually implies a *judgement* about the purposes and intentions of the act, for example in order to distinguish teaching from indoctrination. (I return to the question of purpose below.)

A second distinction relevant for the discussion is between teaching as *task* and teaching as *achievement* (see, for example, MacMillan & Nelson 1968). This distinction goes back to the work of Gilbert Ryle who, in a more general sense, distinguishes between *task verbs* such as to race, to seek, and to reach, and *achievement or success verbs* such as to win, to find, and to grasp (Ryle 1952). Using this distinction we can say that using the word "teaching" to refer to the task does not necessarily imply that the task will lead to success, i.e. that it is followed by the achievement. To say "I taught him Latin for years, but he learnt nothing" (Peters 1967, p. 2) is a correct way of using the word "teaching" in the task-sense of the word. If, on the other hand, we were to shift to the achievement-sense, we would probably say something like: "I *tried* to teach him Latin for years, but he did not learn anything." These considerations have led several authors, such as Israel Scheffler and B. Othanel Smith, to the stronger claim that conceptually teaching does *not* imply learning. This idea is known in the literature as the "standard thesis" (see Noddings 2012, p. 49; see also Komisar 1968). But what, then, might the intention of teaching be, if it is not learning?

To answer this question, we need to look at another set of ambiguities, this time connected to the word "learning". In the English language – and it will be interesting to explore how this works in other languages – "learning" is used both to refer to a *process* and to the *outcome of the process*. To use the word "learning" in the second sense (as achievement in the terms introduced in the previous paragraph) is not very contentious as long as we do not think of it in terms of a product – achievement is a better term here. Although there is a significant body of literature that deals with the complexities of definitions of learning (for an overview and discussion see, for example, Hodkinson, Biesta & James 2008), many authors agree with a basic definition of learning as any more or less durable change that is not the result of maturation. This definition highlights that learning is not about *any* change on the side of the one learning, but about change that has some permanence. And it makes a distinction between change that is the result of the interaction of individuals with their environment, and change that is just the result of biologically or genetically "programmed" processes. What it is that actually changes when we say that people have learned is a question for further elaboration. It can, for example, be change in knowledge, or in ability, or understanding, or behaviour, or emotion, and so on.

Many authors would also agree that what actually brings about learning so understood is what students *do* (albeit there are some further issues in relation to this assumption to which I will return below). Should we therefore also use the word "learning" to refer to what students *do* – which would be using learning also as a task-word? This is actually a more unhelpful use of the word, and in my view a significant degree of confusion in discussions about learning stems from using the word to refer to both an activity and the result of the activity. We can already see a problem with using the word "learning" to refer to an activity in the situation where a teacher would say to students: "For the next half hour I want you all to learn" – as students will most likely ask "But what do you want us to *do*?" This has led Gary Fenstermacher (1986, p. 39) to suggest that the idea that teachers convey or impart some content to their students – which is one way of saying that teaching brings about learning – is actually mistaken. Rather, the teacher "instructs the student on how to acquire the content from the teacher, text, or other source" (p. 39).

Fenstermacher has therefore argued that what teachers should aim for – and thus what the intention of teaching should be – is what he has suggested to refer to as "studenting", similar to what B. Othanel Smith calls "pupilling" (see Fenstermacher 1986). With the notion of studenting, Fenstermacher is able to say in a much more precise manner what the act of teaching is about, namely that of:

> instructing the learner on the procedures and demands of the studenting role, selecting the material to be learned, adapting that material so that it is appropriate to the level of the learner, constructing the most appropriate opportunities for the learner to gain access to the content [...], monitoring and appraising the student's progress, and serving the learner as one of the primary sources of knowledge and skill. (Fenstermacher 1986, pp. 39–40)

By making the distinction between studenting and learning in this way, Fenstermacher not only introduces concepts that allow us to say with much more precision what teachers should intend to bring about. He also makes it possible to identify much more clearly who in the educational relationship is responsible for which part of the process, and therefore who can be held accountable for what. He explains this as follows:

> On this new scheme, the teacher is held accountable for the activities proper to being a student (the task sense of 'learning'), not the demonstrated acquisition of content by the learner (the achievement sense of 'learning'). Thus a learner who fails a reasonably valid and reliable test of content covered in instruction must accept a major share of the responsibility for this failure. To the extent the student lacks the skills of studenting needed to perform well on this test, is given no opportunity to exercise these skills, or is in no helpful way encouraged to engage the material to be learned, the teacher must accept a major share of responsibility for the student's failure. (Fenstermacher 1986, p. 40)

The notion of "studenting" thus helps to create some distance between teaching and learning, albeit that for Fenstermacher the outcome of the act of studenting is still described as learning – which explains why he refers to the person doing the studenting as a "learner" rather than as a "student" (on this distinction see also Biesta 2010c). Komisar (1968) went one step further when he not only stated explicitly that "learning is not what the 'teacher' intends to produce" (p. 183), but also suggested that the intention of teaching might better be captured in terms of the "awareness" of an "auditor" – not a learner or student for Komisar – *"who is successfully becoming aware of the point of the act* [of teaching]" (p. 191; emphasis in original).

What I have established so far, then, is that we should neither think of teaching as the cause of learning, nor think that teaching is necessarily aimed at bringing about learning. I have also shown that there is no necessary *conceptual* connection between "teaching" and "learning". With Fenstermacher we might say, therefore, that learning – as task and as achievement – is "of the learner", and that what teachers should try to bring about is not the learning itself, but the activity of studenting. In this set-up learning is, at most, the "effect" of the activity of *studenting*, but not of the activity of teaching. And this is a helpful insight for indicating with more precision what teachers can be held responsible and accountable for, and what not.

Having created some distance between teaching and learning, the next question is how much learning we actually need or should want in education. This brings me to the second step in my argument.

The Problem with Learning: The "Learnification" of Education[1]

Whereas authors such as Fenstermacher provide a strong argument against the idea that teaching should aim to bring about learning, he nonetheless still sees learning as the last step in the process, in that ultimately the studenting of students should result in their learning. It is with regard to this suggestion that I need to highlight some further problems with the role and status of learning in relation to teaching and education more generally. The first issue has to do with a phenomenon to which I have elsewhere referred as the "learnification" of educational discourse and practice (see particularly Biesta 2009a, 2010a). "Learnification" refers to a relatively recent trend to express much of, if not all of, what there is to say about education in terms of a language of learning. We can see it in the tendency to refer to students, pupils, children, and adults as "learners", to refer to schools as "learning environments" or "places for learning", and to see teachers as "facilitators of learning". The redesignation of the field of "adult education" into that of "lifelong learning" is a further example of the rise of the "new language of learning" (Biesta 2009a), as is the ubiquity of the phrase "teaching and learning".

The main point I wish to make here is that the language of learning is *insufficient* as an educational language. This means that to say that the point of education is that students learn or, with reference to Fenstermacher, that students' studenting should result in learning, is simply not precise enough. In its shortest formula the issue here is that the point of teaching, and of education more generally, is never that students "just" learn, but always that they learn *something*, that they learn it for particular *reasons*, and that they learn it *from someone*. The problem with the language of learning is that it is a language that refers to processes that are "open" or "empty" with regard to content and purpose. So just to say that children should learn or that teachers should facilitate learning, or that we all should be lifelong learners, actually says very little, if it says anything at all.

Unlike the language of learning, a language of education always needs to pay attention to questions of *content, purpose,* and *relationships.* The danger with the rise of the language of learning in education is that these questions are no longer asked, or that they are already taken to be answered (for example according to the suggestion that the only relevant content is academic content, that the only relevant purpose is academic achievement, and the only relevant relationship is for teachers to train students so that they generate the highest possible test scores, for themselves, their school, and their country).

Of the three dimensions – content, purpose, and relationships – the question of purpose is in my view the most important and fundamental question, because it is only once we have been able to indicate what it is that we seek to achieve through our educational activities and endeavours, that we can make decisions about the appropriate content students should engage with, and that we can decide how educational relationships can be used most productively and meaningfully. Yet, as I have suggested elsewhere (Biesta 2010a), what distinguishes education from many other human practices is the fact that it doesn't work in relation to only one purpose, but actually functions in relation to a number of "domains of purpose".

The argument is relatively simple and starts from the observation that in all instances of education – both at the "big" level of national curricula or school systems and at the "small" level of teachers working with their students – education is always about the presentation and acquisition of some content (knowledge, skills, dispositions), but always also introduces students to particular traditions and ways of doing and being and, in addition, has an impact on their formation as a person (either positively, for example by giving them knowledge, skills, and connections to networks that empower them, or negatively when, for example, they are being told to "know their place"). In more theoretical language education thus always functions in relation to three domains: that of *qualification,* that of *socialisation,* and that of what I prefer to refer to as *subjectification,* which is about the ways in which students can be(come) subjects in their own right and not just remain objects of the desires and directions of others.

If it is the case that all education always *functions* in relation to these three domains, then it is reasonable to ask for teachers and others who are involved in the design and execution of education to take explicit responsibility for the potential impact of their work in each of the three domains. This means that qualification, socialisation, and subjectification not only appear as three *functions of education,* but also as three *domains of educational purpose* – three qualitatively different domains with regard to which we need to state and justify what it is we seek to achieve with our students, and what we seek our students to achieve.

Although qualification, socialisation, and subjectification can be distinguished, it is important to see that they cannot be separated from each other. This means, on the one hand, that even schools that claim only to focus on qualification are still impacting in the domains of socialisation and subjectification. It means, on the other hand, that teachers and others involved in education are always faced with finding a *meaningful balance* between the three domains, bearing in mind that what can be achieved in one domain often limits or intervenes with what can be achieved in the other domains (think, for example, of the problematic impact of an excessive focus on achievement in the domain qualification on the other two domains).

All this shows why it is unhelpful to suggest that the point of education is just that students should learn, or that teaching should bring about learning (either directly or via the studenting or pupilling of their students). Without an indication of what it is that should be learned and, more importantly, what something should be learned *for* – the question of purpose – the language of learning is unable to provide a sense of direction, which is precisely where its deficiency as an *educational* language lies.

Being a Learner: Politics and Identity

If the previous section has indicated problems with regard to the *language* of learning, I also wish to discuss some issues that have to do with the *existence* of the learner, that is, with the question of what it means to be or to exist *as a learner*. These questions partly have to do with the politics of learning (for this phrase see Biesta 2013b) and partly with the identity of the learner. Let me start with the politics of learning.

One reason why the language of learning has gained in popularity and prominence may have to do with the fact that learning is increasingly being seen as something natural, and hence as something *inevitable*, that is, as something we do all the time and cannot *not* do. With regard to lifelong learning John Field (2000, p. 35) has argued, for example, that learning is an "unavoidable biological fact [and that] we learn as we breathe, all the time, without giving it any thought". From the idea that learning is something natural, inevitable, and unavoidable, it is only a small step to hear policymakers say that we therefore *must* learn, and this message is indeed increasingly being spread around the globe. Here is, for example, a statement from the UNESCO report on the 2010 *Shanghai Forum on Lifelong Learning*:

> We are now living in a fast-changing and complex social, economic and political world to which we need to adapt by increasingly rapidly acquiring new knowledge, skills and attitudes in a wide range of contexts. An

individual will not be able to meet life challenges unless he or she becomes a lifelong learner, and a society will not be sustainable unless it becomes a learning society. (Yang & Valdés-Cotera 2011, p. v)

This is but one example of a strategy where learning is being used – and perhaps we could even say: hijacked – to pursue a very specific political agenda that is likely to serve a particular segment of society with regard to very specific interests. In this quotation learning appears to be put in the service of a global capitalist economy that is in need of a flexible, adaptable, and adjustable workforce. In this context learning is depicted as an act of *adaptation*, without even hinting at the possible need for asking *what it is* that one is supposed to adapt to and *why* one is supposed to adapt to this, before one "decides" to adapt. Gone are the individual's "freedom to learn" (Rogers 1969) and an understanding of learning in the service of democracy (for example Faure et al. 1972). Instead, learning seems to have become a duty from which there is really no escape – which gives an ironic undertone to the word "lifelong" in the idea of lifelong learning.

The foregoing provides a clear example of the dynamics of the "politics of learning", where political problems, such as questions about the economy, employment, and social cohesion, are turned into learning problems, and where individuals are tasked with solving these problems through their learning (and often also at their own cost). While there are situations where the request or demand for learning is entirely legitimate – we rightly want people to have driving lessons before they drive a car or be properly educated before they practise medicine – the demand to learn should not become all-encompassing. After all, there are also situations where the demand to learn is inappropriate or unjustified as we should not be willing to adapt and adjust to just any situation. And there are situations where there is actually nothing to learn, such as with regard to the question of who, in a democracy, can have a voice, which has to do with one's (legal) status as a citizen, not with one's apparent ability to pass a citizenship exam (see Biesta 2011a).

If this gives an indication of how particular political forces are "positioning" us as learners and of why it might be important not immediately and automatically to accept such positioning, the other point I wish to discuss has to do with the more general identity of "the learner", that is, with the question of what it means to exist *as a learner*. This is a complex discussion because at one level there are many different definitions and conceptions of learning (Illeris 2008) and it may not be possible to bring them all under one rubric or even to identify a common denominator. Nonetheless I wish to suggest that one strong tendency in contemporary conceptions of learning is to see learning as an act of *comprehension* – that is, as an act of sense-making, of gaining knowledge and understanding about the world "out there" (which can either be the natural world or the social world). We can think of the underlying "gesture" of this as a hermeneutical gesture where the world appears to me as something I try to bring to my understanding.[2] While the task of understanding is ongoing – each hermeneutical cycle adds to and modifies our existing understanding, thus providing a new starting point for the next cycle, and so on – learning as comprehension none-theless puts us in a very specific way in the world and in relation with the world.

One could say that acts of understanding and interpretation always start from where we are – they are issued by the self, so to speak – go out to the world, and in some way then return to the self. Learning as comprehension thus puts the self at the centre and makes the world into an object of the self's comprehension. When we look at the etymology of comprehension we not only find the idea of grasping ("prehendere") something in its totality ("com"). The Latin word "hendere" actually has the same root as "hedera", the Latin name for ivy, which invokes the image of a building overgrown by ivy up to the point where the ivy can even destroy the building.

I am playing with these words and images in order to highlight that learning as comprehension puts us in a very particular way "in" the world and in relation to the world. While there is obviously a place for this way of being in and with the world, the point I wish to make is that if this is the *only* way in which we con-ceive of our relation with the world and our position in it, we are significantly limiting our existential possibilities, that is, our possibilities for existing in and with the world. One important limitation of the idea of learning as comprehen-sion is that it puts the self at the centre and turns the world into an object for the self. This can turn into a powerful act where it becomes increasingly difficult for the world – and it is important to bear in mind that the world is both the natural and the social world – to speak on its own terms, as a world that addresses me, speaks to me, interrupts me, limits me, and de-centres me, rather than that it "accepts" that I am already the centre and origin of the relationship. This hints at a rather different relationship between the self and the world, where the first question for the self to ask is not "How can I understand?" but is perhaps closer to something like "What is this asking from me?"

I am not suggesting that it is the one or the other – that we either are in the centre and "out" to comprehend, or that we are out of the centre, trying to figure out what is being asked from us. But I am suggesting that if our main understanding of learn-ing is that of a centred act of comprehension, and if we are further suggesting that this is the natural and inevitable way to be, then we end up in a situation where such a conception of learning and such a learner identity begin to limit our existential possibilities, our opportunities for being in and with the world. This may be a further reason for not immediately or automatically assuming that learning is good and desirable and that the learner identity is "the way to be" and "the *only* way to be".

Construction, Reception, and Being Addressed: Existential Possibilities

Before I turn to the question of whether any of this can make a difference in the practice of teaching, I wish to briefly allude to some of the philosophical discussions that play in the background of what I have said so far. These discussions partly have to do with the status and nature of knowledge, which is the domain of epistemology or theory of knowledge, and partly with existential questions, that is questions about the ways in which we understand our being in and with the world. With regard to the question of knowledge there is an ongoing discussion within the history of philosophy between the idea that knowledge comes from "within" – usually referred to as rationalism – and the idea that knowledge comes from "outside" – usually referred to as empiricism. There are radical empiricists who believe that the mind is a "blank slate" (John Locke) and that *all* knowledge comes from the outside. There are also radical rationalists who believe that all knowledge is basically already "in the mind" and that learning and coming to know are basically processes of recollection (this was, for example, Plato's view).

In this discussion there are, on the one hand, references to situations where our senses are obviously misleading – the classic example being that of the stick in the water, which appears broken when partly in the water, but straight when outside of the water or when totally immersed in it – and, on the other hand, references to situations where we strongly feel that we know something but can never perceive it – such as, for example, the idea of causality (a point made by David Hume, who pointed out that we can see regularity and correlation, but can never observe underlying causal "mechanisms"). The work of Immanuel Kant is commonly understood as a synthesis of empiricism and rationalism through his famous dictum that percepts without concepts are blind, and concepts without percepts empty.

From Kant there is a more or less direct line to constructivist theories of knowing and learning – particularly the work of Jean Piaget and Ernst von Glasersfeld – that have become highly influential in contemporary education (see Richardson 2003) and actually have contributed significantly to the rise of the language of learning and the redefinition of teaching as facilitation of learning. The founding intuition of constructivism is that knowing and learning are processes in which knowers and learners actively construct their knowledge and understanding – they *make* sense – rather than that this is a process where knowers or learners passively receive such knowledge and understanding (for an overview see Roth 2011, particularly chapter 1). The more popular interpretation of this intuition is the suggestion that we can only learn, make sense, and understand *for ourselves*, and that no one else can do this for us. While this intuition is, in itself, correct, it does not resolve the underlying epistemological issues, as what we do "for ourselves" can of course still be understood in terms of construction or reception. Nonetheless this cluster of ideas has strongly motivated the turn towards "the learner" and his or her activities and has, in the same "move", discredited the idea of didactic teaching, and perhaps of teaching altogether (on this problematic see also Biesta 2012b).

I have no space here to go into epistemological detail, not only because of the complexity of the discussion, but also because the discussion is still ongoing, and because there is a body of work emerging that is actually challenging the constructivist "hegemony" in education by highlighting, for example, that all knowing actually stems from a fundamental passivity and receptivity rather than that it is the result of the activity of an intentionally constructing mind (on this point see Roth 2011; for a wider overview of the discussion see Gordon 2012; see also Biesta 2017, particularly chapter 7). What is important for the line of thought in this chapter is that these different understandings of what it means to know are related to very different conceptions of what it means to be "in" the world. They are related to very different modes of existing and thus open up very different existential possibilities. Let me briefly indicate the differences at stake.

The idea of knowledge as a process of construction comes with a conception of human existence akin to what I have said before about the act of comprehension. Construction puts the knower-constructor at the centre of the world to be known, and thus puts the world – natural and social – in the position of object: an object of *my* construction, *my* understanding, and *my* comprehension. Existentially we can think of this as an act of mastery where through my act of knowing I try to master the world. This attitude is particularly visible in the technological engagement with the world where, through the development of technologies, we try to control and master the world. Here, in a very fundamental sense, my existence "occurs" before the existence of the world: I assume that I am there first in order *then* to start making sense of the world. It also means that I assume that the world exists *for* me, that is, that the world is in some way at my disposal as an object for me to make sense of and construct knowledge about.[3]

To think of knowing as an "event" of reception rather than as an "act" of construction positions us very differently in relation to the world. In a sense we could say that to think of knowing as reception is exactly the opposite of thinking of knowing as construction. When we think of knowing as reception the world does not appear as an object that is at our disposal but rather as "something" that comes to us. Knowing then is not an act of mastery or control – our attitude to the world, natural and social, is not technological – but can perhaps better be described as a process of listening to the world, of having a concern for the world, of caring for the world, and perhaps even of carrying the world (see what I have said in chapter 1 on "Auftrag" and "opdracht"). The most important differences here are between activity and passivity – or in slightly different terms: between intentionality and receptivity – and between the world as an object at my disposal (an object for me to do something with) and the world as an object with its own "objectivity" or, with a slightly more precise word: its own integrity.

Whereas construction and reception provide us with two different ways in which we relate to the world, it could be argued that they only differ in how we *relate* – as constructors or receivers – but that in both cases the assumption still is that *we*, in some sense, exist before the world, so that from that position we can start constructing or receiving. This suggests that there are at least further existential possibilities to consider in relation to how we understand ourselves and the world. If construction and reception both assume the existence of a self who either constructs or receives, there is at least one other way of understanding the relationship between self and world, namely one where the world in a sense comes "before" the self, and the self emerges from this "encounter".

This, as I have shown in the previous chapter and will explore further in the next chapter, is captured in the idea that our existence as subject is precisely not in our hands, is not generated from the inside out, so to speak, but emerges in response to an address, in response to an experience of being addressed or being spoken to by what or who is other. It is particularly important here to ponder the difference between *listening* and *being addressed*. Whereas listening starts from the self who opens his or her ear in order to listen, the experience of being addressed comes from the "outside" to us, and in a sense "asks" us to respond. (On the educational implications of the difference between "listening" and "being addressed" see also Biesta 2012a.)

There is, of course, more to say about different understandings of knowing and different understandings of what it means to be in the world. By indicating a number of possibilities – a number of *existential* possibilities – I have at least tried to show that our being in the world can be understood in a number of different ways, and is not necessarily tied to learning and its logic. These are not just theoretical options but possibilities with important practical implications. Think, for example, of the way in which the technological attitude towards the world has not just generated many benefits, but also lies at the heart of many of the ecological problems we are currently facing. Similarly we can say that in domains concerned with our relationships with others – such as ethics and politics – an attitude of mastery and control will generate very different relationships than an attitude of listening, caring, or being spoken to. So what, then, might this mean for education?

Teaching without Learning: "Adopting a Concept"

So far I have tried to show that the relationship between teaching and learning is not a necessary relationship and that the ideas of learning and the learner are not without problems. This means that at the very least we should no longer assume that learning and being a learner are always simply good and desirable. I have also shown how learning as an act of comprehension puts us in a very particular relationship with the world, and that other relationships are conceivable, possible, and perhaps even desirable. While this may suggest that there are good reasons for wanting to "free" teaching from learning, at least to open up other existential possibilities for our students, the question is whether any of this is possible in practice. Is it possible, in our work with students, to take learning "out"? And if we do so, if we teach without aiming for learning, would this still amount to something that is educationally meaningful? In this section I wish to share some experiences from a course I taught a couple of years ago in which I indeed did try to take learning "out".

The course in question was a two-week seminar for doctoral students in education and was organised around an exploration of seven key educational concepts taken from my book *The Beautiful Risk of Education* (Biesta 2014). The concepts were creativity, communication, teaching, learning, democracy, emancipation, and virtuosity. After an introduction we devoted a daily session to each of the concepts, exploring their history, their meaning, and their significance and relevance. At one level I invited the students to explore connections between the concepts and their own research projects so that their understanding of the concepts could grow and deepen, and they might be able to incorporate some of these insights into their own work. Doing so is a rather common way of proceeding in a doctoral course like this, where the assumption is that not everything that is being discussed in the course will be relevant for what the students are doing. Students can, in other words, be selective in what they seek to learn from a course like this.

Yet at that point I reminded the students that education is perhaps not just about growing and deepening what is already there – such as their emerging understanding – but that education can also be understood as an encounter with something that is radically new, something that students precisely do *not* already have. We could think of this as an encounter with something that comes to you without reason, so to speak, because if it is something that is really new, that really comes from the outside, students may not yet have any anchor points for connecting to what is coming to them, and may therefore not (yet) be able to see the reason of what is coming to them. The new that is coming to them may therefore feel more like a burden that needs to be carried than as an insight that is already familiar or that can easily be incorporated into or added to what students already know and understand. I suggested to the students that something like this can happen in education as well, that is, that you encounter something that comes to you rather than that you go towards it – trying to grasp, trying to understand, trying to comprehend – so that it indeed presents you with a burden you can either choose to carry with you for a while, or not. And if you decide to carry it, you may, over time, perhaps develop a relationship with it and perhaps even a desire for it. Who knows?

Against this background I introduced[4] an additional organising principle for the course, namely that of "adoption", as I felt that the idea of adoption came closest to this very different experience of encountering something that comes to you from the outside, as something strange over which you do not have much control or choice, but which, if you decide to stay with it, you may develop a relationship with. So instead of asking the students what is usually asked in courses such as this, that is, to try to understand and make sense of the concepts we were discussing and incorporate them into the "reason" of their own research projects, I asked the students to adopt one of the concepts. And I meant this quite literally. I invited them to let one of the concepts into their lives. I asked them to live with one of the concepts for two weeks and, at the end of the two weeks, provide me and the other students with a report on the adoption experience, that is, a description of what had happened whilst trying to live with the concept for the two weeks. I did not ask them, therefore, to show their understanding of the concept – I did not ask for any comprehension – but tried to open up a different existential possibility for them vis-à-vis the concepts of the course.

I did not force the students to do so – at least I do not think I did – but did say that if they were up for this experiment, then we should take the idea of adoption seriously from the start. To take adoption seriously meant first of all that the students would not be able to *choose* the concept they wanted, but should rather declare a willingness to adopt one of the concepts and then see what would occur. After all, when you are willing to adopt a child, there is also little choice over the very child you adopt, not just because the actual arrival of the child tends to appear quite sudden – a phone call in the evening, a child on your doorstep at 7 a.m. the next morning, and either a "yes" or a "no" from you – but also because, as with every child, you never know what the child will become, which means that you take a responsibility upon yourself for something you cannot really foresee (I return to the theme of the unforeseen in chapter 5). At the end of the first session I therefore left little pieces of folded paper on a table with one of the concepts written on each of them and invited the students to pick one up and let this concept into their lives.

Almost all students did this – there was one student who already had set eyes on a particular concept, and I told the student that this was absolutely fine as well – and over the course of two weeks we proceeded in a fairly conventional manner, exploring and discussing the intricacies and complexities of each of the concepts during our daily sessions. In the sessions we did work on questions of understanding and sense-making – and in this sense the sessions were exercises in comprehension, one might say – although in the background of all this the students were carrying their concept. I do not have any knowledge of what happened with the students and their concepts over the two-week period, and also never had a desire for wanting to know all this, but I do want to share some reflections on the final session, the one where I invited the students to share as much or as little as they wanted about their experience with the concept.

It was first of all interesting to see that it wasn't easy for all students to just give up their identity as a learner and shift to a rather different way of existing in relation to the course and its content.[5] Several of the reports that the students presented were more "traditional" attempts at making sense of the concept, exploring its meaning and significance, and revealed less about what it had meant to encounter the concept, to live with the concept, to carry the concept – in short: to exist with the concept. I pass no judgement on this, but just note that the identity of learning-as-comprehension appears to be quite deeply entrenched, so that to shift out of this identity is easier said than done. I have already hinted at the fact that I deliberately tried to take the moment of choice away from the course by suggesting that the students would let a concept find them, rather than that they could choose the concept. In most cases students were open to this.

Again I do not wish to make any judgement about this, other than highlighting that choice has also become a central part of the modern learner identity and is therefore something that also requires some effort to let go of.

For most students, however, the concept had become a reality in its own right more than just a concept, and the accounts they gave of both the initial encounter with "their" concept and the subsequent time they spent with it were fascinating, and in some cases also quite moving. Some students had encountered the concept that already very much was "their" concept. For example, the student who had encountered the concept of emancipation told how the question of emancipation had always already been a major life-theme; the encounter with the concept was, in this regard, a remarkable affirmation of the importance of this theme or, to put it slightly differently, another encounter with the theme. Other students also spoke about the remarkable fit between themselves and the concept they had encountered.

There were also students for which things worked exactly in the opposite direction, such as the student who had secretly hoped *not* to encounter the concept of "learning", yet this was the very concept that "arrived". The student recounted how she had put the concept – or actually the little piece of paper on which I had written the concept – deep down in her backpack. But for the whole two weeks she could feel it sitting there, as a physical presence, as a burden she had to carry, as something that seemed to be wanting something from her. Another student told about a similar aversion at the moment of the encounter with the concept, and the difficulty of establishing a relationship with the concept – the student told that the concept was left downstairs during the night, but made its presence felt very strongly – although over time the relationship with the concept did change.

These examples not only showed that the concepts were not "just" concepts, and in many cases came to exist in the lives of the students as realities, as things cherished or hated, as things that called out to them, that addressed them, as things that wanted to have a place in their lives, albeit for some students it was easier to accommodate them, that is, to provide them with accommodation, than for others. What also happened in these cases was that the encounter with the concept and the request to adopt the concept moved students "beyond" the traditional learner identity, moved them away from comprehension, to very different ways of being in and with the world. That comprehension became less central for the students was nicely demonstrated by a student who, when we had an informal gathering after the last session, asked me about something I had said earlier in the course. The question was prefaced by saying "I didn't understand it, but I'm not really concerned about that" and then I was asked just to repeat what I had said so that, I think, it could once more be encountered.

I wish to suggest that the students' experiences with the adoption of a concept were significant, not because they gained a deeper understanding of the concept – that was, after all, the very thing that we tried to keep out – but because the request to adopt the concept opened up different existential possibilities for them, different ways of being in and with the world than the default mode of understanding. The request to adopt a concept asked the student to give up some control over the world. It asked them to let something into their lives over which they had little choice and about which they had little knowledge as to what was going to arrive. And it asked them to take care of what came into their lives, even in those cases where they had no particular warm feelings and in some cases even a real dislike for what entered into their lives.[6] By keeping the students away from comprehension – by asking them *not* to learn, *not* to interpret, *not* to make sense – it positioned the students differently in the world and allowed them to experience a different way of existing, of being in and with the world. This was not only valuable in itself, but by interrupting the default tendency to comprehend, it also showed the students that learning is not the only meaningful way in which teaching can proceed and education can take place.

In Conclusion

In this chapter I have tried to argue that the relationship between teaching and learning is neither a necessary relationship, nor is it always automatically a desirable relationship. In addition I have provided a brief example of what can happen if students are specifically asked to refrain from learning. All this is not meant to discredit learning or to argue that there should be no place for learning in education, but to highlight that learning is not the be-all and end-all of education, rather it is only one of the existential possibilities that teaching can aim for. Freeing teaching from learning, showing that *teachingandlearning* is *not* one word, is not only important in order to show that learning is a very particular and in a sense rather limited way in which we can engage with and exist in the world. Freeing teaching from learning, keeping learning out of the classroom, is also important for opening up other existential possibilities for students, particularly possibilities that do not put them and their sense-making at the centre of the educational process, but rather allow them to encounter what comes to them from "beyond" their sense-making, that is, as I have put it, without reason. Something that addresses them, that speaks to them, that may ask something from them, that may call them, that may call them forth, and thus may call their grown-up subject-ness into the world.

Notes

1 I apologise to readers who have encountered the ideas presented in this section before – they are, however, an important step in my overall argument.
2 I discuss my reasons for referring to this as a hermeneutical gesture in more detail in chapter 3.
3 Roth (2011, pp. 5–10) discusses this as the problem of "intellectualism" of contemporary constructivism.

4   It is actually more accurate to say that the notion of adoption came to me, was given to me, so to speak. It was just that I was typing the course outline and wrote "I will then ask all students to adopt one of the concepts" when the word "adopt" turned back to me and started to reveal a different (existential) possibility than just being a posh alternative for the word "choice".

5   There is of course also the question of what happened to me as a teacher.

6   It is tempting, of course, to replace the word "concept" with the word "child" or "student".

3

THE REDISCOVERY OF TEACHING

So far I have taken two steps in my attempt at developing an argument for the rediscovery of teaching. In chapter 1 I have formulated the principal task – or if one wishes: responsibility – of education and educators as that of arousing the desire in another human being for wanting to exist in the world in a grown-up way, that is, as subject. I have indicated what this entails, why it might be meaningful to approach education in this way, and what it asks from the teacher, highlighting the role of interruption, suspension, and sustenance, and the trans-formation of (relationships of) power into (relationships of) authority. I have argued that to exist in the world in a grown-up way means that the question of whether what we desire is what we ought to desire, whether what we desire is desirable, has become a "living question" in our lives, a question we carry with us and consider in every situation we encounter.

In chapter 2 I have discussed the relationship between teaching and learning, arguing that the gap between teaching and learning is bigger than what is nowadays often assumed. I have not only argued that learning, understood as an act of comprehension, denotes only one existential possibility, only one way of being in and with the world, but have also suggested that for that reason there ought to be more to teaching than just learning. Through a discussion of an example where I asked my students to refrain from learning, I have shown that when teaching is "freed" from learning, other existential possibilities begin to open up – existential possibilities that carry significance for our endeavours at existing in and with the world in a grown-up way.

In this chapter I pursue some of the main themes from the previous chapter in more detail, focusing particularly on the question to what extent our existence as subject can be understood in terms of sense-making, understanding, and com-prehension. Against the idea of the human being as a meaning-making organism,

I follow Emmanuel Levinas in his suggestion that our existence as subject is precisely *not* to be approached in terms of (our) comprehension and (our) sense-making, but emerges in other ways and from "elsewhere", so to speak. I connect this to the question of teaching, suggesting that teaching is not a limitation of the freedom of the student (see also chapter 4), but the very way through which the student-as-subject may emerge.

What Is Actually Wrong with Traditional Teaching?

Over the past twenty years or so a rather common argument has emerged in many research publications and policy documents about teaching. What can be found again and again is the idea that so-called "traditional" teaching – that is, a staging of education where the teacher speaks and students are supposed to listen and passively absorb information – is seen as bad and outdated, and where something allegedly more modern, focused on the facilitation of students' learning – either individually or in some kind of dialogical process – is seen as good, desirable, and "of the future". While the opposition between "traditional" and "contemporary" is itself already a bit stale, we should also not forget how traditional the critique of traditional teaching itself actually is. John Dewey already made the point, as did Jan Ligthart in the Netherlands, and many educators and educationalists in many countries around the world before and after them. The critique is also not entirely valid, because even in classrooms where teachers speak and students sit quietly, a lot of things are actually happening on the side of the students. They may of course feel bored, alienated, and ignored, but they may also feel challenged, fascinated, and inspired; who knows? I also wonder whether anyone has actually ever suggested that education *operates* as a process of transmission and passive absorption, even if it is *staged* in this way (see Biesta 2004). Here I fully agree with Virginia Richardson's observation that "students also make meaning from activities encountered in a transmission model of teaching" (Richardson 2003, p. 1628).

In light of the critique of traditional teaching it is, of course, also ironic that some of the currently most popular technology-mediated forms of education – such as TED talks, MOOCs (Massive Open Online Courses), and the numerous professional and amateur instructional videos on YouTube – are staged in "conventional" ways, that is, with someone talking and explaining so that others can watch, listen, and learn. One could even ask whether the endless stream of worksheets and individual and group tasks that have invaded the contemporary classroom – from pre-school to higher education – is not beginning to trivialise education, just turning it into busy work. And we should not forget those momentous examples of traditional, one-directional forms of communication – from Socrates's apology, via Lincoln's Gettysburg address, to the speeches of Barack Obama – where, to my knowledge, no one has actually ever complained about the absence of study questions or group work that would allow the audience to make personal sense of what has been said. In this regard I believe that we really should not underestimate our capacity to receive.

What these observations begin to suggest is that there actually may be something wrong with the ongoing *critique* of traditional teaching. But making this point and trying to establish a more general case for the recovery and rediscovery of teaching is, as I have explained in the prologue to this book, fraught with difficulties. This, as mentioned, is not least so because nowadays the most vocal arguments for teaching and the teacher come from the conservative end of the political spectrum, where they are aimed at re-establishing the kind of order and control that apparently is lacking in modern society and modern education (for a different take on this issue see Meirieu 2007). This seems to suggest that the only *progressive* alternative lies in the demise of the teacher and "traditional" teaching and a turn towards learning – a turn where the teacher only exists as a facilitator of otherwise "autonomous" learning processes.[1]

The problem here, if I see it correctly, has to do with the binary construction of options, that is, with the idea that the only meaningful response to authoritarian forms of teaching lies in the abolition of teaching and a turn towards learning. What remains remarkable is that the third option, namely that of reconstructing our understanding of teaching and the teacher along progressive lines, is little considered. Yet it is in this third option – an option which relies on the idea that freedom is not the opposite of authority or an escape from authority, but has to do with establishing a "grown-up" relationship with what may have authority in our lives; a process in which authority becomes *authorised*, as Meirieu (2007, p. 84) has put it – that we can see the beginnings of an entirely different response to authoritarian forms of teaching.

In this chapter I focus on what we might term the anthropological[2] dimensions of the discussion, that is, the underlying assumptions about human beings and their place in the world. I embark on this with some trepidation, because I think neither that anthropology is a matter of choice – it is not that we can simply choose how we want to understand the human being and then can happily proceed from there – nor that anthropology is a matter of grounding – where, once we know what the human being really is, we can put education on a safe and secure path (on these problems see Biesta 2006; also Biesta 1999).

My ambition with this chapter is to make visible what the prevailing conception of the human being is – particularly in our educational imaginary, but the impact is a wider one – and to suggest that such a conception is neither necessary nor inevitable by indicating how the human being and its place in the world might be approached differently. I deliberately use the word "approached" here because, as I will argue in what follows, this is not a matter of *understanding* the human being differently; the challenge rather is an existential one. Through this I not only seek to create the possibility for developing a different understanding of teaching, but I also seek to show how teaching – or, to be more precise: the experience of being taught (Biesta 2013a) – reveals something important about our human existence.

This will allow me to suggest that in the demise of teaching and the teacher there is actually more at stake than only an educational problematic and a problematic that would only concern the school.

The underlying structure of my argument is fairly simple, but I admit that the detail is more complex. I start from the contention that to the extent to which the critique of traditional teaching is a critique of teaching as control, this critique is educationally valid as it shows that in traditional teaching the student can only appear as an object of the teacher's interventions, but never as a subject in its own right. I then argue that the suggestion that we can overcome this problem by focusing on students and their learning – understood as acts of interpretation and comprehension – fails, because such acts of interpretation and comprehension have an egological structure that not only emanates from the self but also returns to the self, even if this occurs "via" the world. For this reason I suggest that in acts of interpretation and comprehension there is a risk that the self can still not appear as subject, but remains an object in relation to its environment. What I suggest in more philosophical terms, therefore, is that our subject-ness is not constituted through acts of signification. I take this insight from the work of Emmanuel Levinas, who provides the main source of inspiration for this chapter. With Levinas I suggest that our subject-ness is rather called forth from the "outside" – which is why I discuss the theme of "transcendence" – and has to do with the "event" of "being addressed". It is in this event that a different meaning of teaching manifests itself, and it is this sense of teaching that I seek to (re)discover in this chapter.

Overcoming the Egological Worldview

I proceed in this chapter by means of a reading of two texts from Emmanuel Levinas, the philosopher who, in my view, has contributed most to exposing the limitations of the egological worldview, that is, the way of thinking that starts from the (assumption of the existence of the) self as self-sufficient ego or consciousness, in order *then* to thematise everything that is "outside the subject" (Levinas 1994). However, Levinas's thought is not a simple reversal of this gesture but comes closer to what elsewhere I have referred to as an "ethics of subjectivity" (Biesta 2008). The idea of an ethics of subjectivity hints at a double shift. It first of all indicates that Levinas seeks to approach the question of human subjectivity through ethics rather than through knowledge. There is, in other words, no *theory* about the subject, no cognitive claim about what the subject *is*. Yet this also means, and this is the second shift, that Levinas's writings should not be read as a traditional ethical philosophy or theory of ethics that seeks to describe or prescribe what being ethical and acting ethically is. What is at stake in Levinas's ethics of subjectivity is the question of human subject-ness, the question of what it means to exist *as subject*.

Rather modestly – particularly compared to the rich flow of language through which Levinas tries to capture something of the mystery of human subject-ness – Levinas writes that he "describe[s] subjectivity in ethical terms" (Levinas 1985, p. 95). Key in this effort, as I have already alluded to in chapter 1, is his suggestion that responsibility is "the essential, primary and fundamental structure of subjectivity" (p. 95). He emphasises, however, that responsibility here "does not supplement a preceding existential base" (p. 95). It is not that the subject first exists – as a self-sufficient, egological subject – and *then* encounters a responsibility or takes a responsibility upon itself. It is rather, as Levinas puts it, that "the very node of the subjective is knotted in ethics understood as responsibility" (p. 95). Responsibility, in the very useful words of Zygmunt Bauman (1993, p. 13), thus appears as "the first reality of the self". It is the moment where the self finds itself, so to speak. Or to be even more precise: it is the moment where the self *matters* because in its responsibility the self is "non-interchangeable" (Levinas 1985, p. 101).[3]

That Levinas's ethics of subjectivity is not to be understood as a theory about the human subject already indicates some of the difficulties with trying to overcome egological ways of thinking and being. After all, if we simply were to issue a different theory or different truth about the subject – for example by arguing that the self has a social origin – we would decentre the self at the level of our theory but would still be doing so from a centre, that is, the centre from which we issue such a theory. We would therefore performatively assert – "that there is a centre from which I can issue the truth" – the very thing we would declaratively deny – "that no such centre exists". Before I discuss how Levinas engages with this predicament, I wish to say a few things about what I see as a prevailing trend in contemporary views about education, particularly in order to show the role of egological assumptions.

On Robot Vacuum Cleaners, Learning Environments, and the Hermeneutical Worldview

One way in which we might characterise the prevailing educational imaginary is in terms of robot vacuum cleaners. The suggestion that robot vacuum cleaners make something visible about current thinking in and about education came to me after a conversation with a scholar working in the learning sciences who raised questions about my critique of the language of learning – a critique which, to a certain degree, he read as a critique of the very idea of learning itself (which I think is correct, as I have tried to explain in chapter 2). What, so he asked, could be wrong with the study of intelligent adaptive systems? While I was happy to concede that nothing is wrong with the study of such systems *as such*, my question was whether such systems provide us with an adequate image of students in educational relationships. And when I tried to imagine what intelligent adaptive systems look like, the robot vacuum cleaner was the first image that came to mind. And perhaps it came to my mind because in French these machines are known as "aspirateurs autonome" – and it was particularly the word "autonome" that captured my (educational) attention. So what do robot vacuum cleaners reveal about the prevailing educational imaginary?

What is interesting about robot vacuum cleaners is, first of all, that they are indeed able to perform their task – hoovering a room – autonomously, that is, on their own. But what perhaps is even more interesting is that over time they can become more efficient at doing so, because they can adapt – intelligently – to the particular room in which they are performing their task. If their pattern is at first rather random or, to be more precise, guided by the particular algorithm they were programmed with, over time it becomes more adjusted to the environment in which they are operating. We can say, therefore, that robot vacuum cleaners can *learn* or, if we wish, we can say that they can adapt to their environment in an intelligent way. While their learning is autonomous in that the vacuum cleaners can do this without any intervention from the outside, this does not mean that their learning cannot be influenced. The way to do this, the way to let them learn more and different things, is by putting the robot in a different environment so that it needs to adapt to differing environing conditions. One can even assume that robot vacuum cleaners that have adjusted to a range of different rooms become more effective at that task of adapting themselves, that is, adapting to any new environment they are placed in. While their learning remains a lifelong task – each new situation may pose new challenges and thus will require further intelligent adaptation – they may nonetheless become more skilled and efficient at adapting to new situations.

I believe that the foregoing account provides a fairly accurate picture of *a*, and perhaps even *the* prevailing, contemporary educational imaginary. This is an imaginary that sees education as a learner-centred endeavour, where it is ultimately for learners to construct their own understandings and build their own skills, and where the main task of teachers is to provide arrangements in and through which such processes can happen. In this situation the teacher does, indeed, no longer transmit anything but designs learning environments for students in order to facilitate their learning. Similarly, students are not engaged in passive absorption but in active adaptive construction, and it is through this that they acquire the skills and competences that make them more able at adapting to future situations. This also shifts the meaning and position of the curriculum, which no longer exists as the content to be transmitted and acquired, but becomes redefined as a set of "learning opportunities" in and through which students, in a flexible and personalised way, pursue their own unique learning trajectories.

It is perhaps important to note that while this imaginary is contemporary – by which I intend to say that it is shaping contemporary educational practice in many contexts and settings – its theoretical frame is not new. We can find it, for example, in the theory of autopoietic systems, that is, of systems that are able to regenerate themselves in constant interaction with their environment – an idea that was developed in biology by Humberto Maturana and Francis Varela (see e.g. Varela, Maturana & Uribe 1974; Maturana & Varela 1980) and further developed by Niklas Luhmann in his theory of social systems (Luhmann 1984, 1995). A key insight of Luhmann's work is that autopoietic systems (such as human individuals) cannot participate in each other's autopoiesis – which means, for example, that they cannot take part in each other's adaptive activities or cognitive constructions – but that they can "appear" in each other's environments so as to have an *indirect* effect on each other's autopoiesis. Perhaps the most famous example of the way of thinking that underlies the ideas outlined previously can be found in the work of John Dewey, whose understanding of action, communication, and learning is indeed based on a view of the human organism as being in constant transaction with its environment, constantly trying to establish a dynamic equilibrium through processes of doing and undergoing, to use Dewey's phrase (see e.g. Biesta & Burbules 2003; Biesta 2009b; and for Dewey's philosophical account Dewey 1925). And in Dewey's work we can indeed find the claim that "we never educate directly, but indirectly by means of the environment" (Dewey 1966[1916], p. 19).

If I were to characterise the underlying anthropology, that is, the underlying view about the human being and its relationship to the world, I would suggest to call this a hermeneutical anthropology and, more widely, a hermeneutical worldview.[4] The reason for using these phrases is that the human being appears here first and foremost as a sense-making being, that is, as a being who is in relationship with the world – natural and social – through acts of interpretation and comprehension. Such acts are issued from the self and, "via" the world, return to the self. They are acts of comprehension in the literal sense of the word, in that, as I have also discussed in chapter 2, they try to grasp ("pre-hendere") the world in its totality ("com"). In such acts of comprehension, in such hermeneutical acts, the world thus appears as an object of our sense-making, our understanding, and our interpretation.

One could, simply and straightforwardly, affirm that this is how things really are. One could, in other words, argue that the hermeneutical worldview is *true*, and that we should therefore build our understanding of knowledge and communication, but also of ethics, politics, and education, upon this premise.[5] But one could also pause for a moment and ponder whether the hermeneutical worldview is as inevitable as it would seem, perhaps by asking what is *not* conceivable within the confines of this worldview.

There are two questions I would like to raise. One is whether in the hermeneutical worldview the world, natural and social, *can speak* in its own terms and on its own terms. The second is whether in the hermeneutical worldview we can be *spoken to*, that is, whether we can be addressed. The hermeneutical worldview, so I wish to suggest, seems to preclude these two options and it is important, as I will try to make clear in what follows, to see them as two *different* limitations of the hermeneutical worldview. The reason for this lies in the fact that the hermeneutical worldview depicts a universe that is *immanent* to my understanding, to acts of my comprehension that always aim to bring the world "out there" back to me. While such acts of comprehension do have an object – hermeneutics is not phantasy or pure construction – this object always appears as an object of *my* signification and in this sense remains dependent on *my* acts of signification. In the next two sections I take up these two aspects of the discussion – the question of immanence and the question of signification – through a discussion of two short but complex texts from Levinas.

An Opening in an Opening: On Signification and Sense

In his essay "Signification and Sense" (in Levinas 2006),[6] Levinas explores both the limitations and the conditions of possibility of signification, broadly conceived as acts of meaning-making. One line in the rich argument Levinas puts forward concerns what he refers to as the "anti-Platonism in contemporary philosophy of signification" (Levinas 2006, p. 18). This anti-Platonism, which he sees in Hegelian, Bergsonian, and phenomenological philosophies of signification, concerns the claim that, as he puts it, "the intelligible is inconceivable outside the becoming that suggests it" (p. 18). It is the idea that: "There does not exist any *signification in itself* that a thought could reach by hopping over the reflections – distorting or faithful, but sensible – that lead to it" (p. 18; emphasis in original). Or in slightly more concrete language, it is the idea that: "All things picturesque, all the different cultures, are no longer obstacles that separate us from the essential and the Intelligible [but are] the only possible paths, irreplaceable, and consequently implicated in the intelligible itself" (p. 18).

Levinas thus describes a situation of total *immanence*, where all our meaning-making, all our signification, occurs *inside* culture and history and derives its meaning from such cultural and historical contexts or frameworks. He characterises this as anti-Platonic because for Plato "the world of significations *precedes* the language and culture that express it" (emphasis added) so that it remains "indifferent to the system of signs that can be invented to make this world present to thought" (Levinas 2006, p. 18). Plato, so Levinas argues, believed in the existence of "a privileged culture [that] can understand the transitory and seemingly childish nature of historical cultures" (pp. 18–19) – a privileged culture that, so we might say, could give sense *to* signification and make sense *of* signification. Levinas suggests that in contemporary philosophy of signification this option is no longer considered to be possible. What we find instead is a "*subordination* of intellect to expression" (p. 19; emphasis added), that is, a situation where everything we can say or express has to be expressed in and through existing cultural and historical discourses and contexts and gains its meaning from such discourses and contexts.[7]

For Levinas this not only poses a *philosophical* problem, which has to do with the question of where signification gets its meaning or sense from (I will return to this later). It also poses a *practical* problem, which has to do with the question of how communication is actually possible (to which I will return as well). And it poses an urgent *political* problem, because, as Levinas puts it, this "most recent, most daring and influential anthropology keeps multiple cultures on the same level" (Levinas 2006, p. 20). According to Levinas the contemporary philosophy of signification thus amounts to cultural and historical *relativism*. Because of its total immanence, its total embeddedness in and reliance upon existing cultural and historical "framings", contemporary philosophy of signification lacks a criterion that would allow us to make a judgement about the "quality" of differing acts of signification so as to be able to distinguish between those that "make sense" and those that do not "make sense".[8] According to Levinas, contemporary philosophy of signification simply "takes satisfaction [*se complait*] in the multiplicity of cultural significations" (pp. 25–26), which manifests itself as a "refusal of engagement in the Other" (p. 26). Yet it is precisely in the latter "movement" that Levinas sees an opening.

There are two dimensions to how Levinas constructs his argument here, and along both lines he seeks to establish two points. The first is that signification "is situated *before* Culture" and the second that it is "situated *in* Ethics", so that ethics is the "presupposition of all Culture and all signification" (Levinas 2006, p. 36; emphasis added; capitals in original).[9] Rather than refusing engagement in the other it is precisely this engagement which, according to Levinas, is the origin of sense in that it provides an "orientation" (p. 26). In a first step Levinas characterises this orientation "as a motion from the identical toward an Other that is absolutely other" (p. 26). This orientation which, as Levinas puts it, "goes freely from Same to Other" is what he refers to as "a Work" (p. 26; capitals in original). Yet for the Work to be radically other-centred it "must not be thought as an apparent agitation of a stock that afterward remains identical to itself" – which is Levinas's way of saying that engagement in the other[10] should not leave the self unaffected or unchanged – nor must it be thought "as similar to the technique that [...] transforms a strange world into a world whose otherness is converted to my idea" (p. 26) – which I read as another way of describing what, on p. 30, I have called the hermeneutical "gesture", bringing what is other into *my* understanding. That is why Levinas insists that the Work needs to be understood as "*a movement of the Same toward the Other that never returns to the Same*" (p. 26, emphasis in original).

This line of thinking, which is akin to Derrida's analysis of the gift (see e.g. Derrida 1992a, 1995), leads Levinas to such observations as that the Work not only requires "a radical generosity of movement" from the one who "does" the Work, but, because of this, it also demands "*ingratitude* from the Other" (emphasis in original), in that the other is not supposed to "return" the Work by being grateful for it, as this would bring the Work back into a circle of economic calculation of costs and benefits, of expenses and returns (Levinas 2006, pp. 26–27). Levinas writes: "As absolute orientation toward the Other – as sense – the work is possible only in the patience that, pushed to the limit, signifies that the Agent renounces contemporaneity with its fulfilment, that he acts without entering the Promised Land" (p. 27). It is a giving without expecting anything back for what is given. The word that Levinas eventually suggests for this work is *liturgy*, which "in its first signification means the exercise of an office that is not only totally gratuitous but requires from the executant an investment at a loss" – and it is this "uncompensated work", the work we do without receiving or even expecting a return, which Levinas names as "ethics itself" (p. 28).

Liturgy, Need, and Desire

If liturgy is work that is really done without any returns, without anything coming back to us, then it is also important, so Levinas argues, that we do not think of it as something that fulfils some kind of need we would have – such as the need to do good or to care for the other – as in such a case the fulfilment of the need would be the "return" we receive. In this context Levinas introduces the notion of desire (see Levinas 2006). Yet here desire is not to be understood as desire for fulfilment, which is why Levinas writes: "The Desire for Others – sociality – arises in a being who lacks nothing or, more exactly, arises beyond all that could be lacking or satisfying to him" (p. 28). In desire the ego goes out to the other "in a way that compromises the sovereign identification of the Ego with oneself" (p. 28). Desire so conceived is therefore non-egological.

But how should we "approach" this "desire for others that", according to Levinas, "we feel in the most common social experience" (Levinas 2006, p. 30)? Levinas observes that "All analysis of language in contemporary philosophy emphasizes, and rightfully so, its hermeneutic structure" (p. 30), that is, that our approach to the other is to be understood as an act of signification, an act through which we try to understand and make sense of the other. Levinas, however, is after a "third option" where the other is neither "collaborator and neighbour of our cultural work of expression [nor] client of our artistic production, but *interlocutor*; the one to whom expression expresses" (p. 30, emphasis added). Precisely here we find a first and crucial "opening", in that Levinas suggests that signification is not an egological act, it is not a gesture through which the ego generates meaning, it is not self-generated expression "onto" a world. Signification is, in other words, *not* hermeneutics because "before it is a celebration of being, *expression is a relation* with the one to whom I express the expression" (p. 30, emphasis added).

This other "who faces me" is precisely for this reason "not included in the totality of being that is expressed", because in that case the other would be the "product" of my signification, it would be my construction. The other rather arises "behind all collection of being, as the one to whom I express what I express" (p. 30). That this is so, Levinas argues, is because it is only through the presence of the other as *interlocutor* that "a phenomenon such as signification [can] introduce itself, of itself, into being" (p. 30). That is why, as interlocutor, as the one to whom I express the expression "and whose presence is already required so that my cultural gesture of expression can be produced", the other is "neither a cultural signification nor a simple given" but rather "primordially, *sense*" (p. 30, emphasis in original). Here we have to remember that "sense" for Levinas is precisely that which gives our signification meaning and, going on from this, gives our life direction. Levinas emphasises that this "turn" – about which I wish to say one more thing below – "means returning in a new way to Platonism" (p. 38) because it allows us to go beyond "this saraband of countless equivalent cultures, each one justifying itself in its own context" (p. 37). While Levinas praises Husserl for a similar achievement that would allow "for ethical judgements about civilizations" (p. 37), he notes that "One is not obliged to follow the same path Husserl took", which was that of "postulating phenomenological reduction and constitution […] of the cultural world in the intuitive transcendental consciousness" (p. 37). Levinas suggests that there is a different avenue towards "the rectitude of signification", namely through the idea that "intelligible manifestation is produced in the rectitude of *morality* and in the Work" – understood as liturgy (p. 37, emphasis added).

A Second Opening

What Levinas is beginning to suggest, therefore, is that signification is not the "first reality of the self", that, to put it differently, we should not conceive of ourselves as sense-making animals or learners, but that sense-making only "makes sense" in the encounter with the other. For Levinas this encounter is fundamentally an *ethical* encounter, that is, an encounter where there is something "at stake", and where I, that is, my subject-ness, my existing-as-subject, am/is at stake. Before I draw this section to a conclusion, however, there is one more aspect of Levinas's line of thought that needs to be brought in; a line which responds to the point raised earlier about the question of how communication – or with Levinas's term: interlocution – is possible. It has to do with the question of how the other actually can be an interlocutor, and it is here that I would suggest that a second opening takes place.

While Levinas acknowledges that the manifestation of the other – and the word manifestation should be taken literally, that is, as the way in which the other manifests itself – "is of course produced […] in the way all signification is produced", that is, through an action of my "comprehension of the Other" which, as Levinas emphasises, is "a hermeneutic, an exegesis" (Levinas 2006, pp. 30–31), the Other does not just come to me as a product or a result of my signification. After all, if that were the case – if the other were only to appear because I make the other appear through my signification – then signification would remain the original event even if this signification were to have an ethical quality, for example, coming from my intention to want to do good to the other or care for the other.[11] In addition to the appearance of the other as *phenomenon*, as product of my signification, there is also the "epiphany of the Other" – an epiphany that bears its own significance, "independent of the signification received from the world" (p. 31), as Levinas puts it. The other "not only comes to us from a context but signifies itself, without that mediation" (p. 31). It is this unmediated presence coming to us to which Levinas refers as "face" and it is to the epiphany of the face that Levinas refers as "visitation" (see Levinas 2006, p. 31). Face, so we might say, "breaks through" its signification, that is, through its image. This is a process of "deformalization" (Cohen 2006, p. xxxi) where the face speaks and where this speaking "is first and foremost this way of coming from behind one's appearance, behind one's form; an opening in the opening" (Levinas 2006, p. 31).

But the face does not speak in general – its speaking is not "the unveiling of the world" (Levinas 2006, p. 31). Rather the face speaks to *me*; the face addresses me, the face summons me and "announces thereby the ethical dimensions of visitation" (p. 32). It is precisely here, so Levinas argues, that "Consciousness loses its first place" (p. 32) because "the presence of the face signifies an irrefutable order – a commandment – that arrests the availability of consciousness" (p. 32). A moment of interruption. Levinas emphasises that in this moment consciousness is challenged by the face, but that it is crucial to see that this challenge "does not come from awareness of that challenge" (p. 32) because in that case, again, signification would come *before* the address. That is why Levinas emphasises that it is "a challenge of consciousness, not a consciousness of the challenge" (p. 33). This visitation is therefore "the upset of the very egoism of the Ego" (p. 33). It is important to see, however, that this does not amount to the destruction of the Ego but rather to what we might call a decentring: a decentring through which the "Me/Ego" gains its unique significance. As Levinas explains, the responsibility "that empties the Ego of its imperialism [rather] confirms the uniqueness of the Ego", a uniqueness which lies in the fact "that no one can answer in my stead" (p. 33). And discovering "such an orientation for the Ego means identifying Ego and morality" (p. 33) – and hence the moral "origin" of the Ego-as-subject, which is precisely what I have tried to express in the idea of an ethics of subjectivity.

The Criterion, Communication, and the Origin of Signification

I have followed Levinas's argument in detail in order to show how this line of thought addresses the problems Levinas identifies with what he refers to as the contemporary philosophy of signification. These problems were the question of *sense* – Where does signification get its meaning from? – the question of *communication* – How is communication possible in a radically plural universe? – and the question of the *criterion* – What makes it possible for us to evaluate (systems and traditions of) signification? Levinas's line of thought provides an answer to these three questions, not so much to each of the questions separately but more in an overlapping and interlocking way. One key insight is the observation that signification is not an egological act or accomplishment but consists of a relation with the one to

whom I express an expression, the one to whom expression expresses. Signification thus derives its sense from this particular "event" or "encounter" with
another being. In this relation the other does not appear as object of my signification, but as interlocutor. That is why the "appearance" of the other is a
matter of epiphany. And what appears is not an image of the other – which again
would make the other into the "product" of my signification – but what Levinas
refers to as its face.

It is important to see that just as the face is not the product of *my* signification,
the epiphany of the face is also not a matter of the other's signification of me.
The face does not thematise me; the face does not make me into an object of its
signification. Rather the face *speaks to me*. This speech – and this is crucial as
well – is not a revelation of the other that I am just to receive.[12] The key idea
here is that the face speaks to *me* or, to be more precise: the speech of the face
addresses me (and here we need to emphasise both the fact that the face *addresses*
and that the face addresses *me*, in the singular, and not just anyone, which is why,
in chapter 1, I have referred to all this as a first-person matter). It is an address in
which my imperialism is interrupted, where my consciousness is challenged –
"The face disorients the intentionality that sights it" (Levinas 2006, p. 33) –
where I am called to respond, albeit that I have the freedom *not* to respond to this
call. And it is in this moment, in this ethical event, that the Ego gains its significance, precisely because it appears beyond/before/outside of any signification.

In short, then, *the criterion* that Levinas has been searching for appears here as
ethics; *communication* is not a matter of the exchange of meaning(s) but has its
origin in the address, in the being-spoken-to; and it is in the ethical event of
being addressed *that signification acquires its sense*, that signification becomes possible
or, with the more precise formulation Levinas offers: that signification introduces
itself into being, that it becomes real.

Revelation, Transcendence, and Ethics

Before I return to the question of teaching with which I started this chapter, I wish
to look briefly at another short text from Levinas called "Revelation in the Jewish
Tradition" (Levinas 1989; originally published in French in 1977). In this text
Levinas also provides a critique of the hermeneutical worldview, but in a slightly
different register and vocabulary. Some might say that the text is radically different
rather than slightly different as it deals with a theological question of the possibility
of revelation. I see more continuity between this question and the themes of
"Signification and Sense" as in both cases Levinas is trying to articulate a critique of
immanence and an argument for transcendence, an argument for the idea that not
everything that occurs in our lives is generated through our own acts of sense-
making but that there are "things" that come to us from the outside, so to speak.

That the main theme of the text is the overcoming of immanence is already
clear in the opening sentence where Levinas states that the "fundamental

question" he is addressing "is less concerned with the content attributed to revelation than with the actual fact […] referred to as the Revelation" (Levinas 1989, p. 191). Levinas goes even one step further by arguing that this fact in itself is "the first content, and the most important, to be revealed by any revelation" (p. 191). The very point of revelation *is* its exteriority, that is, the fact that revelation is something that comes *to* us and is not our construction or interpretation. This is why Levinas asks how we can "make sense of the 'exteriority' of the truths and signs of the Revelation which strike the human faculty known as reason" (p. 192); "how can these truths and signs strike our reason if they are not even of this world?" (p. 192).

Part of the answer to this question is given in the idea of "the reader's participation in the Revelation" (Levinas 1989, p. 194). While this may, at first sight, sound like an argument for interpretation that would bring hermeneutics back to the scene, Levinas does not reduce revelation to hermeneutics but has a rather different relationship between revelation and the self in mind. He writes that while "its word comes from elsewhere, from outside [it lives at the same time] within the person receiving it" (p. 194). Levinas is suggesting, in other words, that the only "'terrain' where exteriority can appear is in the human being" (p. 194). But he adds to this that the human being here "does far more than listen" (p. 194). That Levinas does not understand this in terms of hermeneutics becomes clear when he argues that the message that comes from the outside does not come "in order to collide with a reason which is 'free'" but rather arrives "to assume instead a unique shape, which cannot be reduced to a contingent 'subjective impression'" (pp. 194–195). Rather, "The Revelation has a particular way of producing meaning, which lies in its calling upon the unique within me" (p. 195). Revelation, in the language from the previous section, speaks to me or, to be more precise: addresses me, calls me, summons me.

That is why, in a familiar line, Levinas emphasises: "My very uniqueness lies in my responsibility for the other [in the sense that] nobody can relieve me of this, just as nobody can replace me at the moment of my death" (Levinas 1989, p. 202). This allows Levinas to articulate a very different notion of freedom – not the liberal freedom of being able to do what one wishes to do, but being free as "simply [doing] what nobody else can do in my place" so that "to be free" means "to obey the Most High" (p. 202).

This brings Levinas back to the idea of subject-ness as "the very fracturing of immanence" (Levinas 1989, p. 204). But how can this fracturing be understood? We might say that understanding is precisely the way in which this fracturing can *not* be understood because if the fracturing, that which comes from the outside, is "thinkable" then it is already, via a hermeneutical gesture, made "safe" and no longer a fracturing. Levinas observes that the difficulty here "stems from our habit of thinking of reason as the correlative of the possibility of the world, the counterpart to its stability and identity" (p. 205). Could it be otherwise, he asks? "Could we account for intelligibility in terms of a traumatic upheaval in experience, which confronts intelligence with something far beyond its capacity, and thereby causes it to break?" (p. 205).

As long as we think of revelation as the revelation of a truth to reason, then all this does not really make sense. But Levinas sees an entirely different option, the one where "we consider the possibility of a command, a 'you must,' which takes no account of what 'you can'" (Levinas 1989, p. 205).[13] In this case, Levinas argues, "the exceeding of one's capacity does make sense" because the type of reason corresponding to the fracture "is practical reason" (p. 205) which must mean, so Levinas concludes, that "our model of revelation be an ethical one" (p. 206). Here notions such as "prescription" and "obedience" play a role (see Levinas 1989, p. 206). But the obedience Levinas has in mind "cannot be assimilated to the categorical imperative, where a universal suddenly finds itself in a position to direct the will" (p. 206). It rather derives "from the love of one's neighbour, a love without eros, lacking self-indulgence, which is, in this sense, a love that is obeyed" (p. 206).

This "love that is obeyed" hints at the possibility "of a heteronomy which does not involve servitude, a receptive ear which still retains its reason, an obedience which does not alienate the person listening" (Levinas 1989, p. 207). It is, in other words, *not* an argument for saying that we should simply receive everything that comes to us from the outside; we still retain responsibility for what we "let in" and for how we respond to what arrives. Levinas is aware that "such moves towards acknowledging an irreducible transcendence" cannot occur within "the dominant conception of reason held by the philosophical profession today" (p. 207), by which he has in mind what earlier I have referred to as the hermeneutical worldview which starts from the self and conceives of the self's relationship with the word in terms of sense-making. "Nothing can fissure the nuclear solidity of this power of thought," Levinas writes, "a thought which freezes its object as a theme" (p. 207), which grasps its object in its entirety with the risk of destroying the very thing it seeks to comprehend.

This is different from the ethical relationship with the other which, "unlike the exteriority which surrounds man whenever he seeks knowledge [...] cannot be transformed into a content within interiority [but] remains 'uncontainable' [while] the relation is maintained" (Levinas 1989, p. 207). Hence Levinas's solution for the "paradox of revelation" is one that claims that we may find a model for this relation with exteriority "in the attitude of non-indifference towards the Other [...] and that it is precisely through this relation that man becomes his 'self'" (p. 207). Ethics, then, "provides the model worthy of transcendence" (p. 207), one where "the Same − drowsy in his identity" is *awakened* by the Other (p. 209).

The Rediscovery of Teaching

I started this chapter with critical questions about the all-too-common and all-too-facile critique of traditional teaching − a critique that seems to have become a new dogma of contemporary educational thought. I showed how this critique has led to a demise of teaching and the teacher and a turn towards learning: a turn where the teacher can only exist as a facilitator of otherwise autonomous learning processes. From the "sage on the stage", the teacher seems to have become the "guide on the side" and, according to some, even the "peer at the rear". The reason for the emergence of the turn towards learning seems to lie in the fact that "traditional" teaching is perceived as an act of *control*. That this is so also becomes visible when we look at the motivation of those who, in light of the turn towards learning, are making a case in favour of teaching, because they do so precisely because they want teaching to be a powerful act of control aimed at maintaining or restoring individual and societal order. While order is not necessarily bad – the question is not whether or not we need order, but when and where we need what kind of order and for what purposes; think, for example, of the immense importance of the legal order – the problem with the idea of teaching as control is that in such a relationship the student can never appear as a subject, but remains an object. In a world that is not interested in the subject-ness of the human being this is, of course, not a problem. The question is whether this is a world we should desire.

Yet what emerges from the ideas put forward in this chapter is that the option that is proposed as a response to the idea of teaching-as-control, namely the idea of learning and, more specifically, that of learning as meaning-making or sig-nification, suffers from the same problem in that in acts of signification *the learner also cannot appear as subject*. One way to understand why this is so has to do with the fact that acts of signification are issued from the self and return – "via" the world as I have put it – to the self. Signification thus keeps the self to the self, never interrupted, always already with itself and sufficient for itself. Another way of looking at this is to say that in its ongoing attempts to adapt and adjust to always changing environing conditions the self remains an object vis-à-vis the environment it is trying to adapt to. While such acts of creative adaptation may help the self to *survive* – and it is remarkable how much of contemporary dis-course is about survival, for example about the need for acquiring the skills for surviving in an unknown future – it never results in a possibility for the self to *exist* (also in the literal sense of being outside of oneself). The question that never arises, to put it differently, is whether the environment to which the self is trying to adapt is an environment one ought to adapt to, an environment worth adapting to. The self – and perhaps we should say: the adjusting or adaptive self – can never out of its own generate a criterion with which to evaluate that which it is adjusting to. It is thus "caught", as an "object", by that to which it is adjusting – an issue I tried to make clear with the image of the robot vacuum cleaner.

This is where the "opening" Levinas creates through his critique of the herme-neutical worldview has its significance, as it shows that our subject-ness is *not* constituted from the inside out through acts of interpretation and adaptation, but is called into being from the outside, as the interruption of my immanence, the interruption or fracturing of my being-with-myself, of my consciousness. This, as I have tried to show, is neither the moment where I interpret the other, nor the moment where I listen to the other, and it is also not the moment where the other makes sense of me, and in this regard it is entirely outside of the realm of signification. It rather is *the moment where I am addressed* by the other, where the other, in Levinas's words, "[calls] upon the unique within me" (Levinas 1989, p. 195). *And may not this event of being addressed give us an entirely different and far more significant account of teaching and the experience of being taught?* [14]

Concluding Comments

It is in light of these ideas that we may begin to see why the idea of intelligent adaptive systems such as robot vacuum cleaners precisely does *not* provide us with an adequate image of students in educational relationships. While, as mentioned, such systems can learn, can adapt and adjust to their environments, and can, in this regard, be said to be capable of signification, the very "thing" that cannot happen, the very "thing" that can never "arrive" in their universe, is the address of the other, that is, the event of being taught. *While such systems can learn, they cannot be taught, they cannot receive (a) teaching.*

Here then we encounter an altogether different account of the event of teaching, one that is precisely *not* aimed at control, at the exercise of power, and at the establishment of an order in which the student can only exist as object, but rather one that calls forth the subject-ness of the student by interrupting its ego-centrism, its being-with-itself and for-itself. This is not only a teaching that puts us very differently in the world. We could even say that this teaching puts us in the world in the first place. It is (a) teaching that draws us out of ourselves, as it interrupts our "needs", to use Levinas's term, or, in the vocabulary I have intro-duced in chapter 1, as it interrupts our desires, and in this sense frees us from the ways in which we are bound to or even determined by our desires. It does so by introducing the question of whether what we desire is actually desirable, both for ourselves and for the life we live with what and who is other.

Such teaching is not authoritarian because it does not reduce the student to an object but rather has an interest in the student's subject-ness. But it does not overcome authoritarianism by *opposing* it (which would mean leaving students entirely to their own devices, that is, to their own learning-as-signification). It does so by establishing an entirely different relationship. This is a relationship of authority, because in moving from what we desire to what we can consider desirable, we give authority to what and who is other or, with a slightly different word, we *authorise* what and who is other by letting it be an author, that is, a subject that speaks and addresses *us*.

We have arrived, then, at the option that seems to be absent in the current way in which the critique of traditional teaching is being formulated, namely where the critique of teaching-as-control immediately ends up with the idea of learning-as-freedom. In the preceding pages I have not only tried to argue that a different alternative *is* possible. I have also suggested that a different alternative *ought to be* possible because if we replace teaching-as-control with an alleged freedom of signification, we actually reinforce the unfreedom of our students because in acts of signification students remain with themselves and always return to themselves, never arriving in the world, never achieving (their) subject-ness. These ideas begin to outline a non-egological approach to teaching, an approach that is not aimed at strengthening the ego, but at interrupting the *ego-object*, at turning it towards the world, so that it can become a *self-subject*.

Notes

1 I use "autonomous" here to refer to the idea that these processes are supposed to be going on anyway, irrespective of the presence of the teacher.
2 I refer here to philosophical anthropology, not empirical or "cultural" anthropology.
3 In a recent paper, Zhao (2015) raises some questions about my existential reading of Levinas's approach to the question of human subject-ness. She does this in the context of the discussion about humanism. As I have discussed in detail in Biesta (2006), I see (philosophical) humanism as any attempt to articulate a truth about the human subject, that is, any attempt to define what the human being is. Whether such a definition sees the human being as fixed and self-enclosed or as open, intersubjective, and always in the making, is not the issue that matters. The problem with humanism, in other words, is *not* about which definition about the human subject is preferable, but is about the very idea that it is possible and desirable to define the "essence" of the human subject. This is why I value Levinas's ethical approach, since it doesn't try to define what the human subject is, but seeks to indicate in which situations my subject-ness *matters* – see also chapter 1.
4 The reference to hermeneutics does not "cover" all positions and views that go under this heading. As I make clear later in this chapter, the use of this notion is particularly inspired by Levinas.
5 I am inclined to say that pragmatism – particularly in the work of Dewey and Mead – provides one of the most developed examples of this "programme". This chapter can therefore also be read as an exploration of the limits of the pragmatic worldview and everything that has emerged from this worldview, including a theory and practice of education. For my critique of this "project" see particularly Biesta (2016).
6 A different English translation was called "Meaning and Sense" (see Levinas 2008); the original French version was published in 1964 under the title "La Signification et le Sens".
7 In my discussion of Levinas's thoughts I am trying to stay fairly close to his own formulations, as the language he uses does matter to what he is trying to convey. The main point he is addressing here is what in contemporary discussions is known as the question of cultural or historical relativism, that is, the idea that all we can know (or at least all we can express about what we know) is relative to the particular cultural and historical frameworks in and through which we express and know.
8 The language of "making sense" may sound like the problem is only one of interpretation. This is, of course, not the case. The questions at stake here are ultimately political as they raise the question of whether "systems" such as fascism or Hitlerism (on the term and the issue see Levinas 1990[1934]; see also Critchley 2014) can be criticised in any way or whether the only thing we can say is that within their own premises they make "perfect sense".

9 It is, therefore, the manifestation of the ethical event – or, to be (much) more precise: the epiphany of the ethical demand – that gives sense to signification. This is discussed in more detail in what follows.

10 I have chosen to use "Other" with a capital "O" only in direct quotations from Levinas but otherwise just write it as "other", mainly in order to signify that the encounter with what and who is "other" is a rather everyday experience rather than something special which the use of the capital "O" might suggest. I am aware that the use of the capital "O" is also to mark the distinction between two French words, "autre" and "autrui", where Other with a capital "O" is meant to refer to the latter.

11 This does of course raise important questions for the role of care and the ethics of care. Let me state one more time that the "message" of Levinas's work is *not* that we should care for the other. I would even say that there is no "should" emanating from Levinas's work at all. The "should" can only come from me.

12 I do not have the space in this chapter to engage in detail with the distance between Levinas and Heidegger, but this is one point where this distance appears and where, in my view, Levinas crucially moves beyond Heidegger. While, to put it briefly and crudely, Heidegger and Levinas both see a similar problem with signification – namely that signification is egological, that it is driven by the self and always returns to the self – Heidegger proposes that the alternative to signification is reception, where we receive what speaks to us and care for it, whereas Levinas proposes that the alternative to self-enclosed signification lies in the fact that what speaks to us addresses us, singles us out, and summons a response. Whereas pure receptivity is ultimately criterionless – it has no criterion to "select" or judge what it should care for – Levinas "moves" us from receptivity to responsibility, where the question for me is not how to receive and hold, but to ask what is being asked from me (with the emphasis, once more, on *me* in the singular, not on anyone in general). The distance between Heidegger and Levinas is also the reason why, earlier in this chapter, I identified two different problems with the hermeneutical worldview – not only the problem of how the world can speak in its own terms but also how we can be spoken to.

13 I return to this idea in chapter 5.

14 I make the distinction between "teaching" and "being taught" because a difficult but important issue in this discussion has to do with the question of whether the teacher has the power to teach or whether the event of being taught should be understood as a gift that can be neither fully given by the teacher nor enforced by the student, but may nonetheless arrive in educational relationships (I discuss this in more detail in Biesta 2013a). I also refer the reader to Zhao (2014) for a probing discussion of these ideas.

4

DON'T BE FOOLED BY IGNORANT SCHOOLMASTERS

One place where the rediscovery of teaching may well be most difficult to achieve – at least at first sight – concerns the role of teaching and the teacher in education that explicitly seeks to promote emancipation. There is, after all, a long tradition that sees emancipation precisely as a release – or in stronger language: an escape – from the influence of teachers and educators more generally. From that angle it is at least counterintuitive to assume that teaching and emancipation have something to do with each other. Yet it is this very connection that I seek to explore in this chapter. I take up the question of the role of teaching and the teacher in emancipatory education in conversation with German and North-American versions of critical pedagogy, with the work of Paulo Freire, and that of Jacques Rancière. In each case, as I will show, we cannot only find strong arguments for the idea that education should be aimed at emancipation, that is, at the freedom of those being educated. In each case we can also find clear but quite different views about the role of teaching and the teacher.

My aim with this chapter partly is to show the different ways in which the role of the teacher in emancipatory education can be conceived and how this is related to different understandings of emancipation itself and of the dynamics of emancipatory education. But the motivation for writing this chapter also stems from what I see as a rather problematic uptake of the work of Rancière in recent discussions about emancipatory education, an uptake in which the key message of Rancière's book *The Ignorant Schoolmaster* (Rancière 1991) is taken to be that anyone can *learn* without a teacher and that it is this alleged freedom to learn – the freedom of signification, in the language of Levinas – that would constitute *a* or perhaps even *the* moment of emancipation (for a discussion see Pelletier 2012; Biesta & Bingham 2012; see also Stamp 2013; Engels-Schwarzpaul 2015; and later in this chapter). In what follows I seek to challenge this interpretation of

Rancière's work by arguing that the key message of *The Ignorant Schoolmaster* rather is that emancipatory education is not a matter of transfer of knowledge from a teacher who knows to a student who does not (yet) know, but nonetheless is a process in which teachers and their teaching are indispensable.

What complicates the discussion is the fact that in later work – and here I will particularly focus on Rancière's essay "The emancipated spectator" (Rancière 2009, chapter 1) – Rancière seems to have "forgotten" this message himself and seems to be turning the argument for emancipatory teaching into an argument about emancipatory learning by focusing on the freedom of students and other spectators to construct their own meanings and understandings in the face of the act of teaching.[1] By showing how such a constructivist interpretation goes against what I consider to be Rancière's unique contribution to the discussion about educational emancipation, I will also be able to articulate with more precision why and how teaching is indispensable for emancipatory education and why we should therefore not be fooled into thinking that ignorant schoolmasters, because they have no knowledge to give, have nothing to teach and therefore can be disposed of.

Education as a Matter of Emancipation[2]

The idea that education is not just about the perfection of individuals through their engagement with culture and history – a line of thought particularly prominent in the Greek idea of *paideia* (παιδεία) and in some conceptions of the idea of *Bildung* (for a critical discussion see Klafki 1986; Heydorn 1972) – but ultimately has to do with their existence as autonomous subjects (Drerup 2015) and thus with their *emancipation*, has been part of the modern educational experience at least since Rousseau (Løvlie 2002). If *paideia* was an education *for* free men in order to further their freedom as citizens and in this regard stood in opposition to the education meant for manual labourers and artisans, the *banausoi* (βάναυσοι) (Jaeger 1945), the modern experience came to see education as a process that should bring about freedom rather than that it was only meant for those who were already free. Along these lines education thus became seen as a process of *liberation*.

While some authors were interested in the ways in which education might contribute to such liberation, others made the stronger claim that education is *necessary* for such liberation. The often-quoted opening sentence of Kant's essay "An answer to the question 'What is Enlightenment?'" in which he defines enlightenment as the human being's "release from his self-incurred tutelage", with tutelage or immaturity being described as the human being's "inability to make use of his understanding without the direction from another" (Kant 1992 [1784], p. 90), provides a telling example of the latter approach, particularly when combined with the claim from his essay on education that human beings can *only* become human through education and are nothing but for what education makes of them (see Kant 1982, p. 701[3]).

From here the emancipatory impetus developed along two lines, one that we might call child-centred or psychological, and another that we might call society-centred or sociological. The first followed Rousseau's insight (Løvlie 2002) that adaptation of the child to the external societal order would corrupt the child, which led to the idea that a choice *for* the child could only mean a choice *against* society. This line of thought not only played an important role in the establishment of education as an independent academic discipline in Germany towards the end of the nineteenth and the beginning of the twentieth century (see Biesta 2011b). It also was central to child-centred forms of education that emerged around the time under such names as "progressive education", "Reformpädagogik", "New Education", or "éducation nouvelle". These developments were further supported by theories that conceived of the child as a natural category and a "given", and not as something that had to be understood in social, historical, or political terms.

In the German context the limitations of this understanding of emancipatory education became painfully clear when it turned out that theories and practices that focused exclusively on the child could easily be inserted into a wide range of different ideological systems, including Nazism and fascism (see e.g. Klafki & Brockmann 2003). This is why after the Second World War educators and educationalists in Germany such as Herwig Blankertz and Klaus Mollenhauer turned to Marxist and neo-Marxist thought, including the early work of Jürgen Habermas, in order to develop what in German became known as "kritische Pädagogik" (see e.g. Mollenhauer 1976[1968]). About two decades later, but with precursors in the work of "social reconstructionist" educationalists such as George Counts (see Stanley 1992), a similar strand of work emerged in North America through the work of authors such as Michael Apple, Henry Giroux, and Peter McLaren under the name of "critical pedagogy". As a critical theory of and for education, the emancipatory interests of these forms of critical pedagogy focused on the analysis of oppressive structures, practices, and theories with the ambition to bring about "demystification" and "liberation from dogmatism" (phrases used by both Mollenhauer and McLaren; see Mollenhauer 1976[1968], p. 67; McLaren 1997, p. 218).

The Modern Logic of Emancipation and Its Contradictions

The conception of emancipation that emerges from this line of thinking is one that conceives of emancipation as liberation from the oppressive workings of power. A crucial step in the process of emancipation therefore consists of exposing the working of powers – demystification – because it is assumed that only when we know how power works and how it works upon us that we can begin to liberate ourselves and others from it. What the Marxist tradition added to this – and this, in turn, has had a crucial influence on critical and emancipatory pedagogies – is the notion of *ideology* (see Eagleton 2007). One of the key insights expressed in the idea of ideology is not only that all thought is socially determined, but also, and more importantly, that ideology is thought "which *denies* this determination" (Eagleton 2007, p. 89). The latter claim is linked to Friedrich Engels's notion of false consciousness: the idea that "the real motives impelling [the agent] remain unknown to him" (Engels, quoted in Eagleton 2007, p. 89).

The predicament of ideology lies in the claim that it is precisely *because* of the way in which power works upon our consciousness that we are unable to see how power works upon our consciousness. This not only implies that in order to free ourselves from the workings of power we need to expose how power works upon our consciousness. It also means that in order for us to achieve emancipation, *someone else*, whose consciousness is not subjected to the workings of power, needs to provide us with an account of our objective condition. According to this line of thought, then, emancipation is ultimately contingent upon the truth about our objective condition, a truth that can only be generated by someone who is positioned *outside* of the influence of ideology – and in the Marxist tradition this position is considered to be occupied either by science or by philosophy. This line of thought not only provides us with a particular logic of emancipation – one that sees emancipation as a liberation from oppressive power structures and processes – but also provides us with a particular logic of emancipatory education, one that seeks to bring about such liberation through acts of "demystification" and "liberation from dogmatism", as mentioned earlier.

Key to the modern logic of emancipation is the idea that emancipation requires a particular intervention from the outside by emancipators who themselves are not subjected to the power that needs to be overcome. This intervention takes the form of demystification, that is, of revealing to the ones to be emancipated what their objective condition is. This not only makes emancipation into something that is done *to* someone, but also reveals that emancipation is based upon an assumed inequality between the emancipator and the one being emancipated, an inequality that will only be resolved in the future when emancipation has been achieved or brought about. It is presumably not too difficult to recognise a particular pedagogy in this depiction of the modern logic of emancipation. This is a pedagogy where the teacher knows about the objective condition of the student, where it therefore is the task of the teacher to explain this condition to the student with the ambition that the student ultimately becomes like the teacher or, to be more precise, that students move from a situation of ignorance about their objective position and condition to one of knowledge and understanding, similar to the knowledge and understanding the teacher already possessed. Such a situation may be described as one of equality.

As I have discussed elsewhere in more detail (Biesta 2010b, 2014), the modern logic of emancipation is not without problems and also not without contradictions. One problem is that although emancipation is aimed at liberation of the one to be emancipated, it actually installs dependency at the very heart of the act of emancipation. After all, the one to be emancipated is dependent upon a "powerful intervention" by the emancipator in order to gain his or her freedom. More importantly for the argument in this chapter, this intervention is based on knowledge the emancipator claims to have about the objective condition of the one to be emancipated; knowledge which, before emancipation "arrives", is hidden from the one to be emancipated. This means that the modern logic of emancipation starts from a distrust in the experiences of the one to be emancipated, suggesting that we cannot really trust what we see or feel but need someone else to tell us what is really going on.

Whereas in classical Marxism the Marxist philosopher was supposed to be able to occupy this all-knowing position, in our times we often find psychology and sociology occupying this space, asserting that they can reveal what is really going on in our heads – or more often nowadays: our brains – and in our social lives. Rancière captures well what is going on here by highlighting that under this logic of emancipation we need someone who "lifts a veil off the obscurity of things", who "carries obscure depth to the clear surface, and who, conversely, brings the false appearance of the surface back to the secret depths of reason" (Rancière 2010, p. 4). We should not immediately reject the modern logic of emancipation but should at least try to understand the particular issues it sought to address and the particular "frame" from which it attempted to do so. Nonetheless, the clear tension between the ambition to liberate and the claim that this requires someone telling you what is really going on in your head and in your life may help to explain why an encounter with the modern logic of emancipation, particularly when enacted educationally, may not immediately "feel empowering" (Ellsworth 1989).

Paulo Freire, Emancipation, and the Pedagogy of the Oppressed

The contradictions of the modern logic of emancipation resonate strongly with what Paulo Freire has referred to as "banking education", a mode of education where students are turned into "'receptacles' to be 'filled' by the teacher" and where teaching becomes an "act of depositing, in which the students are the depositories and the teacher the depositor" (Freire 1993, p. 53). The fact that banking education appears to be central to the modern logic of emancipation and emancipatory education raises the interesting question of how Freire's own conception differs from this – a question that is particularly important given Freire's place in the "canon" of modern critical pedagogy (see e.g. Lankshear & McLaren 1994). The critical difference, so I wish to suggest, has to do with Freire's understanding of oppression, that is, of that from which we need to be emancipated.

For Freire oppression is not a matter of one person or group exerting power over another person or group, but rather concerns a situation of *alienation*. Although alienation may well be the result of one person or group exerting unwarranted power over another person or group, the exercise of unwarranted power as such does not constitute the kind of oppression Freire seeks to over-come. Freire rather defines oppression as the situation where human beings *are prevented from being human* – or as he tends to put it: where human beings are prevented from being "more fully human" (Freire 1993, p. 39). This not only explains why Freire characterises liberation as a process of *humanisation*, that is, of becoming more fully human. It also shows why Freire is not after the liberation of the oppressed from the power of the oppressors, but after liberating *both* the oppressor and the oppressed from the inauthentic and alienated way of being in their linked identities of oppressor and oppressed, so that they can "enter the historical process as responsible Subjects" (Freire 1993, p. 18). This is why Freire's pedagogy is not a pedagogy *for* the oppressed, where through a powerful intervention the oppressed are set free, but a pedagogy *of* the oppressed. And Freire emphasises again and again that "the great humanistic and historical task of the oppressed [is] to liberate themselves and their oppressors as well" (Freire 1993, p. 26).[4]

For Freire authentic existence is a way of existing as a subject of one's own actions rather than as the object of someone else's actions. Authentic existence is therefore a matter of freedom. Yet freedom for Freire is not a matter of just doing what one wants to do, but encompasses autonomy *and* responsibility (Freire 1993, p. 29; see also Lewis 2012, pp. 82–86). Moreover, to exist as subject rather than object does not mean that one exists purely for and with oneself. Freire stresses that "World and human beings do not exist apart from each other, [but] exist in constant interaction" (Freire 1993, p. 32). For Freire the interaction between human subjects and the world requires both action and reflection. The "action and reflection of men and women upon their world in order to transform it" is what he calls *praxis* (see Freire 1993, p. 60). Praxis thus characterises the authentic existence as subject, which is why Freire sees it as "the new raison d'être of the oppressed" (Freire 1993, p. 48), that is, *after* they have overcome their alienated way of being.

Freire's understanding of oppression as alienation provides the reason why his critique of banking education is different from common complaints about the transmission conception of education as a conception informed by a deficient theory of learning. Although Freire does argue that banking education leads to superficial forms of learning where "words are emptied of their concreteness and become a hollow, alienated, and alienating verbosity" leading to memorisation but not to real understanding (Freire 1993, p. 52), his critique is *not* that banking education relies on a misguided learning theory so that all problems are resolved if we were to allow students to be active constructors rather than passive recipients. He rather hints at the deeper point that in banking education students can only appear as objects of the acts of the teacher, and not as human subjects in their own right. In banking education "the teacher is the Subject of the learning process, while the pupils are merely objects" (Freire 1993, p. 54). Emancipatory education therefore needs to begin with addressing "the teacher-student contradiction" which, in his view, can only be done "by reconciling the poles of the contradiction so that both teachers and students are simultaneously teachers *and* students" (Freire 1993, p. 53; emphasis in original).

The Roles of the Teacher in Freire's Pedagogy of the Oppressed

Freire's response to the problems of the modern logic of emancipation thus seems to be one that heralds the end of the teacher. After all, in order to overcome the teacher–student contradiction that characterises banking education, both the teacher and the student need to give up the very identity that keeps them in an oppressive and dehumanising relationship. Instead they need to engage in a relationship which Freire calls *dialogue*.

Through dialogue, the teacher-of-the-students and the students-of-the-teacher cease to exist and a new term emerges: teacher-student with student-teachers. The teacher is no longer merely the-one-who-teaches, but one who is himself or herself taught in dialogue with the students, who in turn while being taught also teach. They become jointly responsible for a process in which all grow (Freire 1993, p. 61).

One could say that Freire here dissolves the (oppressive) teacher–student relationship of banking education by turning it into a process of joint learning, joint discovery, joint creation of knowledge, although in Freire's vocabulary it is more accurate to say that banking education is transformed into joint *praxis*, that is, into an authentic human existence for both the (former) oppressor and the (former) oppressed. This is no longer a situation in which the teacher is the one who has knowledge and the students just memorise the content narrated by the teacher. Instead both are involved in collective acts of inquiry, inquiry in "fellowship and solidarity", which are "directed towards humanization" (Freire 1993, p. 66).

In Freire's hands the teacher thus transforms into a fellow inquirer, that is, into someone who, always together with their students, is involved in praxis, that is, in transformational action-reflection. Here the teacher is a subject *with* other subjects, rather than a subject depositing knowledge into objects. In one and the same move students cease to be "docile listeners" and become "critical co-investigators in dialogue with the teacher" (Freire 1993, p. 62). In this situation, Freire argues, "no one teaches another, nor is anyone self-taught" (Freire 1993, p. 61).

While at this level the banking-teacher disappears and the teacher-as-fellow-inquirer emerges, it is important to acknowledge that this is not the only figure of the teacher present in Freire's work. There are at least two more "teachers" to be found in Freire's writings. This raises the interesting question of how these different identities can be reconciled. Key here is to see that the figure of the teacher as fellow-inquirer, as subject involved in praxis with other subjects, describes the situation where the teacher–student contradiction *has been resolved*. It describes, in other words, the situation *after* alienation. But the important question for emancipatory education is not so much what this situation looks like, *but how we might get there* and whether teachers have anything to do in moving towards the situation where the teacher–student contradiction has been resolved.

The first point Freire repeatedly makes in relation to this question is that oppression cannot be overcome through banking education. "The pedagogy of the oppressed cannot be developed or practiced by the oppressors" (Freire 1993, p. 36), because such a gesture – which can take the form, for example, of "false generosity" or "paternalism" – "itself maintains and embodies oppression" (p. 36). This reveals that Freire is well aware of the contradictions that characterise the modern logic of emancipation and their enactment in educational settings and why he maintains that "the great humanistic and historical task" of liberation of both the oppressed and the oppressors lies with the *oppressed* and has to lie with them (p. 26).

But Freire immediately adds that "if the implementation of a liberating education requires political power and the oppressed have none" this then raises the problem of how the oppressed can carry out a liberating pedagogy "prior to the revolution" (Freire 1993, p. 36). Freire's response to this predicament is twofold. Firstly, he makes a distinction between two stages within "libertarian pedagogy", the first in which "the oppressed unveil the world of oppression and through praxis commit themselves to its transformation", and the second "in which the reality of oppression has already been transformed, [so that] this pedagogy ceases to belong to the oppressed and becomes a pedagogy of all people in the process of permanent liberation" (p. 36).

But – and this is the second part of Freire's response – the "pedagogy of the first stage" must deal with another problem too, which is "the problem of the oppressed consciousness" (Freire 1993, p. 37), a consciousness shaped by the very relationship of oppression that needs to be overcome. While Freire highlights that this "does not necessarily mean that the oppressed are unaware that they are downtrodden [...], their perception of themselves as oppressed is [nonetheless] impaired by their submission in the reality of oppression" (p. 27). "Submerged in this reality", Freire writes, "the oppressed cannot perceive clearly the 'order' which serves the interests of the oppressors whose image they have internalized" (p. 44).

The Teacher as "Revolutionary Leader"

So how is it possible to change this situation? This is perhaps the most delicate aspect of Freire's theory, because on the one hand he wants to resist the idea that the oppressed must be told to become subjects of their own history.[5] Yet on the other hand, because the "oppressed consciousness" prevents the oppressed from seeing themselves as subjects of their own history, the oppressed need in some way to be "prompted" to become engaged "in the ontological and historical vocation of becoming more fully human" (Freire 1993, p. 48); they must be "prompted" to "engage in reflection on their concrete situation" on the assumption that "reflection – true reflection – leads to action" so that this is not a matter of "armchair revolution" (p. 48).[6]

Freire adds two points to this. One is that "action will constitute authentic praxis only if its consequences become the object of critical reflection," that is, if they bring about "critical consciousness" (Freire 1993, p. 48). The other is that Freire does give a specific name to those who do the prompting – he calls them "revolutionary leaders" (see e.g. Freire 1993, p. 49) – though he does emphasise that these are not leaders who lead the oppressed out of their oppression, but leaders who are involved, alongside the oppressed, in transformational action-reflection, that is, in praxis. This is why Freire writes that "revolutionary leadership must ... practice *co-intentional* education [where] teachers and students (leadership and people) co-intent on reality, are both Subjects, not only in the task of unveiling that reality, and thereby coming to know it critically, but in the task of re-creating that knowledge," a process through which they discover themselves as the "permanent re-creators" of reality, and thus as subjects of their own history (Freire 1993, p. 51).

In the idea of the "revolutionary leader" we can see a different figure of the teacher at work in Freire's thought, namely of the teacher as the one *who instigates praxis*, not as a powerful act through which the oppressed are liberated from their delusions, but by starting up, in a kind of boot-strapping way, the very transformational action-reflection that characterises the human way of being in the world. While the "revolutionary leader" is close to the teacher-student who works with the student-teachers *after* the revolution, the work of the teacher before the revolution is at least different in its orientation, as it aims to *engage* the oppressed in transformational action-reflection – and in his discussion of problem-posing education (see Freire 1993, chapter 4) Freire describes in much detail how such engaging of the oppressed in praxis might be carried out.

While in this way Freire seems to make an interesting case for a form of emancipatory teaching that does not fall back onto the monological mode of banking education, there is one further level in Freire's work and hence a third figure of the teacher where Freire is less successful in resolving the predicament of emancipatory teaching without banking. This comes into view when we acknowledge that in such books as *Pedagogy of the Oppressed* Freire himself operates as a teacher, not only by telling (other) teachers what they should and should not be doing, but also by expressing strong claims about the allegedly true nature of human beings. After all, Freire defines oppression as the situation where human beings are prevented from being "more fully human", thus implying that to overcome alienation means to be closer to what it means to exist in a (more) fully human way, that is, as responsible subject of one's own history. While Freire's depiction of what it means to be human is not entirely without reason, it is nonetheless a very particular vision of what it means to be human, and therefore perhaps one that not everyone will accept or recognise as what all human beings ought to strive for.

Although Freire's critique of the logic of oppression is original and important, and although the metaphor of banking education, particularly in the way in which Freire uses and develops this idea, provides a powerful reference point for the critique of monological educational practices in which students can only appear as objects, the way in which Freire himself appears as a teacher shows that it is perhaps more difficult to escape from a banking mode of emancipatory education than Freire seems to believe. It is here that Rancière's account of Joseph Jacotot, the "ignorant schoolmaster", seeks to articulate a different response to the contradictions of the modern logic of emancipation and emancipatory education.

Rancière, Jacotot, and the Ignorant Schoolmaster

In *The Ignorant Schoolmaster: Five Lessons in Intellectual Emancipation* (Rancière 1991), Rancière recounts the story of Joseph Jacotot (1770–1840), a French schoolteacher who during his exile in Belgium in the first decades of the nineteenth century developed an educational approach which he called "universal teaching". Jacotot's approach stemmed from a discovery he made when he was invited to teach French to Flemish students whose language he didn't speak. What was peculiar about this situation was that there was "no language in which he could teach [his students] what they sought from him" (Rancière 1991, p. 1). Nonetheless his students did manage to learn to speak and write French, which they accomplished through studying a bilingual edition of Fénelon's novel *Télémaque*.

Rancière's exploration of the "case" of Jacotot is interesting for two reasons, which are both connected to the discussion of Freire. One has to do with the fact that Jacotot and his students did not share a language, so that there was no possibility for Jacotot to deposit any content in the minds of the students. There was, in other words, no possibility for banking education. Yet while in this regard – that is, in terms of the transmission of knowledge – Jacotot wasn't able to teach his students anything, Rancière insists that this didn't mean that Jacotot's students learned without a schoolmaster. Jacotot *did* teach and *did* act as a schoolmaster, albeit an ignorant one (see below). And it is precisely in relation to this point that Jacotot – at least in the hands of Rancière[7] – provides a way of overcoming the Freirean "teacher–student contradiction" that does *not* result in the dissolution of the teacher in the way in which this is the case in Freire. Let me try to explain how this is achieved.

Whereas Freire focused his critique on education as a process of *banking*, Rancière's critique has a slightly different target, as it focuses on the role of *explanation*. Rancière contends that in educational settings explanation offers itself "as a means to reduce the situation of inequality where those who know nothing are in relation with those who know" (Rancière 2010, p. 3). When teachers explain something to their students, they do so with the intention to give their students the knowledge and understanding they do not yet have. In this sense it looks reasonable to think of explanation as the way to overcome the inequality between the teacher who knows and the student who doesn't know *yet*.

Rancière argues, however, that whereas this may be true when we look at the content that is being transmitted from the teacher to the student, the way in which the act of explanation is itself performed communicates something very different, namely that explanation is *indispensable* for learning and understanding, that is, that students are thought to be *unable* to come to understanding *without* explanation. This is the point Rancière makes when he suggests: "To explain something to someone is first of all to show him [that] he cannot understand it by himself" (Rancière 1991, p. 6), which means that to explain is "to *demonstrate* an incapacity" (Rancière 2010, p. 3; emphasis added). Explanation then turns education into what Rancière refers to as *stultification* – a process that keeps students "in their place", that literally keeps them stupid and without a voice – rather than a process of *emancipation*.

Rancière thus suggests that explanation actually enacts and in a sense inaugurates and then perpetually confirms the inequality of teacher and student. In this set-up it is not so much that a student is the one who *needs* explanation. It is rather that the act of explanation constitutes the student as the one who is unable to learn *without* explanation, *without* the intervention of a "master-explicator". This leads Rancière to the conclusion that the student so conceived is actually the *product* of the "explicative order" (Rancière 1991, p. 4), not its condition. The explicative order is founded upon what Rancière calls the "myth of pedagogy", which is "the parable of a world divided into knowing minds and ignorant ones, the capable and the incapable, the intelligent and the stupid" (p. 6). The explicator's "special trick" here consists of a "double inaugural gesture" (p. 6):

> On the one hand, he decrees the absolute beginning: it is only now that the act of learning will begin. On the other, having thrown a veil of ignorance over everything that is to be learned, he appoints himself to the task of lifting it. (Rancière 1991, pp. 6–7)

The intention behind this approach to teaching is generally a laudable one, as the teacher aims "to transmit his knowledge to his students so as to bring them, by degrees, to his own level of expertise" (Rancière 1991, p. 3). The "art" of the schoolmaster, "who methodically lifts the veil from that which the student could not understand alone, is the art that promises the student will one day be the equal of the schoolmaster" (Rancière 2010, p. 5). But will this promise ever be delivered? Is it ever possible to escape from the circle of explanation? Or is it the case that as soon as one starts out on a trajectory of explanation, one will be there forever, always trying to catch up, always trying to understand what the explicator already understands, but always in need of the explicator's explanation in order to understand? Viewed in this way explanation is actually "something completely different from a practical means of reaching some end" but rather appears to be an end in itself. Explanation is "the infinite verification of a fundamental axiom: the axiom of inequality" (Rancière 2010, p. 3).

Rancière's Emancipatory Teacher

The question this raises is whether it is possible to break away from the circle of powerlessness "that ties the student to the explicator" (Rancière 1991, p. 15).

Rancière suggests that this may indeed be possible, but not through the introduction of more "refined" or more "progressive" forms of explanation. Here Rancière clearly diverges from the path of the modern logic of emancipatory education by arguing against the idea that emancipation results from an explanation of the objective condition of the student. He writes:

> The distinction between 'stultification' and 'emancipation' is not a distinction between methods of instruction. It is not a distinction between traditional or authoritarian methods, on the one hand, and new or active methods, on the other: stultification can and does happen in all kinds of active and modern ways. (Rancière 2010, p. 6)

The more fundamental question emerging from this discussion is therefore whether it is possible to teach *without explanation*, and it is here that the case of Jacotot is relevant, because it provides us precisely with an example of this.

Yet what is important about the "case" of Jacotot – and it is here that Rancière and Freire diverge – is that the case of Jacotot is not one where the teacher had completely withdrawn and education had turned into collective learning or collaborative inquiry. It rather provides us with an example of an educational dynamic where students learned without a "master *explicator*" (Rancière 1991, p. 12; emphasis added). Rancière summarises this by saying that "Jacotot had taught them something [but] he had communicated nothing to them" (p. 13). The dissociation of teaching from communication is central for Rancière's argument and provides one way to understand the idea of the ignorant schoolmaster, as the educational dynamic that is at stake here is one that no longer relies on the (superior) knowledge of the schoolmaster. But in what way, then, is the ignorant schoolmaster involved in teaching?

Rancière characterises the shift that is at stake here with the help of the distinction between intelligence and will, in that what Jacotot did was not to replace the intelligence of his students with his own intelligence, but rather to *summon* his students to use their own intelligence. The relationship between Jacotot and his students is therefore not a relationship of intelligence to intelligence but of "will to will" (Rancière 1991, p. 13). From this Rancière concludes that whereas stultification takes place "whenever one intelligence is subordinated to another", emancipation takes place when an intelligence obeys only itself "even while the will obeys another will" (p. 13). What therefore is at the heart of the conception of emancipatory education that emerges from this is what Rancière describes as the act of revealing "an intelligence to itself" (p. 28).[8]

Rancière highlights that the route students will take when summoned to use their intelligence is unknown, but what the student cannot escape is "the exercise of his liberty" (Rancière 1991, p. 23).[9] This is why Rancière concludes that there are only two "fundamental acts" for the schoolmaster: "He *interrogates*, he demands speech, that is to say, the manifestation of an intelligence that wasn't aware of itself or that had given up" and "he *verifies* that the work of the intelligence is done with attention" (p. 29; emphasis in original). What is verified here is not the *outcome* of the use of intelligence, as this would return the process to that of explanation, but only the *use* of intelligence, that is, that the "work" of intelligence is done with attention. Rancière emphasises that this interrogation should not be understood in the Socratic way where the purpose of the interrogation seems to be that of leading the student to a point that is already known by the master. While this "may be the path to learning" it is "in no way a path to emancipation" (p. 29). Central to emancipation, then, is the consciousness "of what an intelligence can do when it considers itself equal to any other and considers any other equal to itself" (p. 39).

Rancière highlights that to start from the assumption of the equality of all speaking beings is not to assume, naively, that equality *exists*. It is not to assume that he has a special insight into how inequality exists and how it can be transformed into equality. Rancière actually writes that about inequality "there is nothing to know" (Rancière 2010, p. 4) – which adds another layer of meaning to the idea of the ignorant schoolmaster.

> Inequality is no more a given to be transformed by knowledge than equality is an end to be transmitted through knowledge. Equality and inequality are not two states. They are two "opinions", that is to say two distinct axioms, by which educational training can operate, two axioms that have nothing in common. All that one can do is verify the axiom one is given. The schoolmaster's explanatory logic presents inequality axiomatically. [...] The ignorant schoolmaster's logic poses equality as an axiom to be verified. It relates the state of inequality in the teacher-student relation not to the promise of an equality-to-come that will never come, but to the reality of a basic equality. (Rancière 2010, p. 5)

The point for Rancière, in short, is not to *prove* the equality of intelligence. "It's seeing what can be done under that supposition" (Rancière 1991, p. 46).

Emancipation, Education, and Teaching

The figure of the ignorant schoolmaster that emerges from Rancière's discussion of Jacotot – and I wish to emphasise one more time that what we are looking at is Rancière's "use" of the case of Jacotot, not Jacotot himself – is important in the context of the question of whether teaching has a role to play in education that aims at emancipation. It is important to keep this focus in mind, that is, to see the figure of the ignorant schoolmaster as having to do with the question of emancipatory education, and not to see it as a paradigm for all dimensions of education.

Rancière's "intervention" is clearly orientated towards the question of how in educational relationships and settings students can appear and exist as subjects rather than objects and towards the question of what this requires from the teacher. Rancière's argument is therefore neither an argument *against* education as the transmission of knowledge or education as explanation – those "modes" of education are perfectly acceptable if the ambition is to transmit knowledge or to bring about understanding – nor an argument for a kind of constructivist classroom in which the teacher is only present as a facilitator of learning but no longer has something to teach and is no longer allowed to teach something.

The point I wish to make here – and this is crucial for what I seek to do in this chapter – is that *Rancière's argument is an argument about emancipation and the role of the teacher in emancipatory education, and not a general theory of education or schooling or the dynamics of instruction (didactics)* (which is why Jacotot's notion of "universal teaching" is misleading where it concerns the way in which Rancière makes use of Jacotot). At a very basic level Rancière's argument is a critique of the idea that emancipation relies upon some deeper insight about our true human existence that, through an act of explanation, needs to be transmitted from the emancipator to the one to be emancipated. In this sense he appears to be in agreement with Freire's insight that banking education can never be the method of emancipation and with regard to this point both Freire and Rancière disagree with a basic tenet of the modern logic of emancipation and emancipatory education, namely the idea that emancipation rests on providing an explanation of the objective condition of the one to be emancipated. But there are three ways in which Rancière's approach differs from Freire's.[10]

One is that Rancière's approach retains a very explicit and precise task for the teacher and therefore also retains a very specific identity for the teacher, albeit not in terms of the transmission of knowledge, but in terms of a relationship at the level of will. Rancière describes the logic of emancipatory teaching in the following way: "The emancipatory teacher's call forbids the supposed ignorant one the satisfaction of what is known, the satisfaction of admitting that one is incapable of knowing more" (Rancière 2010, p. 6). The second difference is that for Rancière equality is not some kind of deeper truth about the human being – which would, as I have shown to be the case with Freire, turn emancipatory teaching back to the transmission of a truth about the true and objective condition of the one to be emancipated. For Rancière equality functions as an assumption, as something that gives direction to emancipatory teaching, not as a truth upon which it is founded but as a possibility that constantly asks for what Rancière terms verification – not to be understood as providing evidence for its truth, but understood in the literal sense of making true, that is, acting as if it were true in order to see what follows from it. This also means, and this is the third point where Rancière's approach differs, that equality is not projected into the future, as a state that will only come into existence "after the revolution" (see Thompson 1997), but is situated in the here and now.

Three Conceptions of Emancipatory Education: Liberation, Truth, and Teaching

Comparing the modern logic of emancipation with the views of Freire and Rancière reveals a number of important differences in how emancipation is conceived and how the role of education – and more specifically the role of the teacher – is understood. According to the modern logic, emancipation is understood as *liberation from power*. As oppression is not just understood in material terms but also in what we might call discursive terms – the idea of ideology – liberation relies on a teacher who provides the one to be emancipated with the non-distorted truth about their objective condition.

Freire and Rancière are both critical of the modern logic of emancipation, but for different reasons and with different outcomes. For Freire the main problem seems to be the powerful position of the teacher, hence he conceives of emancipatory education as a process where the teacher becomes a fellow-inquirer who, together with other fellow-inquirers, is involved in the action-reflection process called praxis. Freire thus takes the teacher out of the equation, albeit that he struggles to do so entirely as he still has a role for the revolutionary leader and, as I have argued, ultimately appears as a teacher himself, making claims about what it means to exist authentically as a human being. This is the reason why he defines oppression as alienation from this authentic existence and sees emancipation as the return to this state of being.

Against this background we can see that Rancière goes in the exact opposite direction, as he gives up on the idea that it is possible or necessary to base emancipation upon a truth about the objective or authentic condition of the human being. But unlike Freire he does retain a key role for the teacher; not, however, as the one who provides the ones to be emancipated with knowledge about their objective or authentic condition – which is the reason why the emancipatory schoolmaster is *ignorant* – but in enacting a particular intervention or interruption (see also Biesta 2009c), one that, as he puts it, *forbids* the ones to be emancipated the satisfaction of claiming that they are incapable of learning, thinking, and acting for themselves. Oppression thus appears as the belief that one is unable to learn, think, and act for oneself – a belief that expresses a denial of one's freedom, a denial of one's ability to exist as subject. Emancipation is about revealing "an intelligence to itself" (Rancière 1991, p. 28) or, in a more precise formulation, interrupting and refusing the student's denial of their own freedom.

Simply put, then, the modern logic of emancipation relies on a teacher and truth, Freire takes out the teacher and ultimately retains the role of truth, whereas Rancière retains the teacher but takes out truth. Since for Rancière emancipation doesn't "run" on a truth to be conveyed from the teacher to the student, the emancipatory teacher is an *ignorant* teacher – not because he possesses no knowledge, but because the logic of emancipation does not rely on it and doesn't "run" on knowledge.

Constructivist Enthusiasm: The Uptake of Rancière

In the foregoing pages I have provided a reconstruction of three different conceptions of emancipation and three different approaches to emancipatory education.
Starting from the contradictions that are present in the modern logic of emancipation
I have presented Freire and Rancière as providing two different responses to these
contradictions. Each takes a different horn of the dilemma posed by the modern
logic of emancipation. Whereas Freire tries to get rid of the authoritarian teacher
who prevents students from appearing as subjects in the educational relationship,
we could say that Rancière gets rid of the role of authoritarian knowledge that
prevents students from being different from how they are being defined by that
knowledge and how they come to define themselves by it, namely as *incapable*. I
have also highlighted that Freire and Rancière introduce different understandings of
oppression and that their views about emancipation respond to those understandings.

My particular interest in this chapter, however, concerns the role, position, and
identity of the teacher in emancipatory education, and it is here that I wish to
locate the unique contribution Rancière has made to the discussion, as he has
managed to highlight a "third option", in which teachers actually have something
important to do vis-à-vis emancipation and are not seen, as was the case in Freire,
as part of the problem. But unlike the idea that teachers should supplant false
consciousness in their students with true consciousness – a manoeuvre that Freire
rightly objects to – Rancière takes the question of emancipation away from
matters of knowledge and truth. We can see this in the two formulations he
provides for the role of the emancipatory schoolmaster. One formulation is
positive in the sense that it indicates what the emancipatory teacher should do,
namely "revealing an intelligence to itself". The other formulation is negative in
that it is about forbidding the supposed ignorant one "the satisfaction of admitting
that one is incapable of knowing more".[11]

What is remarkable about the uptake of Rancière's work in the field of education
is that many seem to have missed the particular edge of Rancière's argument – that
is, that it is an argument about the role of knowledge in emancipatory education
(and, more specifically, a rejection of the idea that emancipation "runs" on
demystifying knowledge) – and have read it as a general discussion about education-
as-instruction rather than a specific discussion of education-as-emancipation.
Moreover, the idea of the ignorant schoolmaster has been read along the lines of
contemporary constructivism, where it seems to have become "common sense"
to claim that in education everything centres around students' learning – their
acts of sense-making or comprehension – and the only thing teachers can do and
should be doing is to facilitate such sense-making.

Pelletier (2012, p. 615), for example, refers to this view when she writes that
"teaching, as all good, progressive teachers know, is not about transmitting
knowledge, but enabling another to learn." Engels-Schwarzpaul (2015, pp. 1253–
1254) makes a similar claim in her discussion of Rancière, when she writes that

"it is now widely accepted that learning is not based on the unilateral conveyance of knowledge from teacher to student" but that it is "more effective when students take an active part in knowledge building". Against this background she takes the key message of Rancière's *The Ignorant Schoolmaster* to be one of "[encouraging] learning through the use of one's own intelligence, experiment and experience, attentiveness and persistence" (Engels-Schwarzpaul 2015, p. 1255), thus turning Rancière's precise "message" about the complexities of emancipatory education into a general theory of instruction.

There is a similar tendency in the account Chambers (2013) gives of Rancière's educational theory. Although strongly focusing on political questions, Chambers, where it concerns matters of education, comes close to a constructivist reading of Rancière as well, suggesting that Rancière "advocates an utterly radical pedagogy" centred around a "rejection of mastery [...] of schoolmasters who know it all, and convey this knowing to their students" (Chambers 2013, p. 639). Chambers thus presents Rancière's "new pedagogy [as] a reversal of the explicative order's primary assumption", suggesting that what is central to this new pedagogy is the students' "ability" to come to their own understanding "without the explanations of a master" (p. 644). He writes:

> When a student picks up a book and reads it for herself (even, as in the case of Jacotot's teaching experiments, a book written in a language other than her mother tongue), then she is using the method of equality. This capacity for anyone to read the book without having someone else telling them what it means – this is the power of equality, and this is all there is to equality. (Chambers 2013, p. 644)

Against readings such as these – which don't promote a full-blown constructivism but do tend to take Rancière's argument as a general theory of education that should put the learning and sense-making of students at the centre – I wish to maintain that Rancière's work provides us with an argument about *teaching* rather than learning and that the "location" of this argument is in the discussion about *educational emancipation*.

The Role of Teaching in Emancipatory Education

With regard to the first point – that Rancière is presenting an argument for teaching not for learning – the claim Rancière makes in *The Ignorant Schoolmaster* is therefore *not* that anyone can learn without a teacher. This is not because Rancière would disagree with this claim – as it stands, it simply is true – but because this is not what the discussion is about. The claim Rancière rather makes (and here he distinguishes himself both from the modern logic of emancipation and from Freire) is, as mentioned, that emancipation doesn't "run" on knowledge (which is why the argument should be read within the confines of the discussion about educational emancipation). It neither runs on a truth about the nature of the human being, nor on a truth about the objective condition of the one to be emancipated. It is for this reason that an emancipatory teacher should not be understood as a teacher who possesses *such* knowledge, which is why the emancipatory teacher is characterised as ignorant.

But, to make the point one more time, this is not because the emancipatory teacher lacks knowledge, but because *knowledge is not the way of emancipation*. Here also lies the significance of Rancière's claim of equality as an *assumption*. Unlike Freire, Rancière doesn't put a strong claim about the authentic existence of the human being on the table – and in this sense he is also explicitly un-Kantian – but articulates an explicitly political interest and an explicitly political project.[12]

When Rancière writes, therefore, that "learning also takes place in the stulti-fiers' school" (Rancière 1991, p. 102), it is precisely to show that emancipation is not a matter of learning. There is not only the point that learning can happen anywhere, with and without a teacher. There is also the point that to "become" emancipated – and it is actually more accurate to say: to *be* emancipated – is not something that requires learning, but is about using one's intelligence under the assumption of equality. Doing so is not to reveal a particular capacity – particularly not the capacity to learn, interpret, or make sense – *but is rather to inscribe oneself in the political project of equality* (see also Biesta 2010b). Of course, in order to use one's intelligence in such a way, no teacher is needed; that is the whole point of using one's *own* intelligence. Yet where the emancipatory teacher has a role is in those cases where students – and I would like to add: of any age – *deny* or *refuse* this option, either by claiming that they are unable to think and act for themselves or by expressing that they are unwilling to think and act for themselves. The emancipatory teacher thus has a role in those situations where students deny or refuse their possibility for being (a) subject and prefer to be or remain (an) object. The particular intervention of the emancipatory teacher is aimed at this "attitude", if that's the appropriate term here – a point to which I return in chapter 5.

Rancière Reading Rancière

There are two more points to add to the discussion, and both have to do with Rancière's own reflections on his work, also in response to the ways others have engaged with it. One has to do with the question and status of explanation, as there seems to be a tendency in those commenting on Rancière's work to highlight the irony of trying to explain what the work is about when the work seems to be quite critical of the logic of explanation. However, as I have tried to indicate in the preceding pages, we should not read Rancière's argument as a case for the prohibition of explanation (on this see also Hallward 2005; Stamp 2013). Rancière is helpfully clear about this himself when he writes that "We can certainly use our status as legitimate 'transmitters' to put our knowledge at others' disposal" and that this is actually what he himself is "constantly doing" (Rancière 2011, p. 245).[13] The only point here is that explanation – and particularly the attempt to explain what's really going on in another person's head or life – is not the way of emancipation.

The second point, however, is more problematic from my perspective, as in later writings Rancière seems to be veering towards a constructivist reading of his own work, one where emancipation becomes understood as the freedom to learn and, more specifically, the freedom to interpret and make sense. In the passage just quoted about legitimate transmitters, Rancière actually continues by saying that "what is 'stultifying' from a Jacotist perspective is the will to anticipate the way in which they will grasp what we put at their disposal" (Rancière 2011, p. 245). This becomes a bigger theme in *The Emancipated Spectator*, originally given as a talk in 2004 and subsequently published as chapter 1 in a book with the same title (Rancière 2009). Although the discussion in this essay is on questions of theatre and the position of spectators, Rancière discusses this as an educational problematic as well, making explicit reference to *The Ignorant Schoolmaster*.[14]

In the rendition of the dynamics of education that Rancière provides in this discussion, he seems to have shifted from a focus on emancipatory teaching to a more general account of education as a teaching-learning situation – or, as I called it earlier in this chapter, a general theory of instruction. And the account Rancière gives here is one that comes close to a constructivist reading, where the dynamic of education is not that of transmission of knowledge from the teacher to the student, but one where students learn through what we might term "trial and error" – in Rancière's words "the path from what she [the student] already knows to what she does not yet know, but which she can learn just as she has learnt the rest" (Rancière 2009, p. 11). Rancière calls this "the poetic labour of translation" – which he claims is "at the heart of all learning" (p. 10). It is translation because it is a process where the student moves from what she already knows to what she does not yet know; and it is poetic because the student does not repeat what is already there, but invests his or her own understanding. As Rancière puts it:

From this ignoramus, spelling out signs, to the scientist who constructs hypotheses, the same intelligence is always at work – an intelligence that translates signs into other signs and proceeds by comparisons and illustrations in order to communicate its intellectual adventures and understand what another intelligence is endeavouring to communicate to it. (Rancière 2009, p. 10)

In this account the teacher also appears in a different way from how I have discussed this above, namely as a facilitator.

He does not teach his pupils his knowledge, but orders them to venture into the forest of things and signs, to say what they have seen and what they think of what they have seen, to verify it and have it verified. (Rancière 2009, p. 11)

What Rancière is describing here, then, is very much an account of learning rather than an account of teaching. Moreover, it is an account of learning in the general sense of making sense or, with the term introduced in chapter 2, of learning as comprehension. And it could be read in constructivist terms, in that each individual – we might even say: each individual learner – constructs his or her own "story", or with the phrase Rancière uses: each individual "composes her own poem" (Rancière 2009, p. 13). One thing Rancière highlights in his account of this dynamic is that there is no direct relationship between the teacher/ performer and student/spectator and therefore neither the ambition (p. 14) nor the possibility for "uniform transmission" (p. 15). There rather is always a "third thing" – the work of art, the theatre performance, a book, "or some other piece of writing" (pp. 14–15) – that is "alien to both" but to which they can refer "to verify in common what the pupil has seen, what she says about it and what she thinks of it" (p. 15). There is, therefore, a radical openness of interpretation in relation to this "thing" – and Rancière does indeed affirm that "in a theatre, in front of a performance, just as in a museum, school or street, there are only ever individuals plotting their own paths in the forest of things, acts and signs that confront and surround them" (p. 16), which provides "starting points, intersections and junctions that enable us to learn something new" (p. 17).

What is most remarkable about *The Emancipated Spectator*, at least from the perspective that I have been pursuing in the previous pages, is that Rancière seems to locate the emancipatory "moment" precisely in the acts of interpretation of spectators – and by implication in the acts of interpretation of students, that is in their alleged "freedom of signification". In relation to the "new idiom" that emerges when artists "construct the stages where the manifestation and effect of their skills are exhibited", Rancière argues that "the effect of the idiom cannot be anticipated" and that it "requires spectators who play the role of active interpreters, who develop their own translation in order to appropriate the 'story' and make it their own story", from which he concludes that: "An emancipated community is a community of narrators and translators" (Rancière 2009, p. 22).

There are two reasons why where Rancière seems to end up here is problematic – one has to do with the role of the teacher, the other with the status of emancipation. The first problem with the constructivist "uptake" of Rancière's work – ironically, also by Rancière himself – is that the unique position he had carved out for the teacher in emancipatory education seems to have disappeared. Rancière rather seems to be "back" where Freire already was, that is, with the teacher as a facilitator of learning, a facilitator of students constructing their own stories. The second problem has to do with the question of whether everyone's freedom to construct their own story – a freedom to which I referred in chapter 3 as the freedom of signification – is a meaningful notion of freedom and hence a meaningful notion of emancipation.

As I explained in chapter 3, I doubt whether this is the case, because the question that immediately arises is what the criterion would be upon which we were to judge the different interpretations, significations, or poems that people would come up with. The freedom of signification thus appears as a kind of neo-liberal freedom – where everyone is free to articulate their own "story" – rather than a political let alone a democratic freedom where there would always be a question about how the different "poems" would impact on the ways in which we live our lives *together-in-equality*, rather than each of us being enclosed in our own story. This is not only remarkable given the fact that the idea of equality plays such a key role in Rancière's writings. It is also remarkable because the figure of the emancipatory teacher that emerges from the reconstruction provided in this chapter precisely depicts emancipatory teaching as an *interruption* of such a relativistic set-up where students would only spin around in their own universe – emancipatory teaching as an interruption of the refusal to exist as subject.

Conclusion: Don't Be Fooled by Ignorant Schoolmasters

In this chapter I have tried to highlight Rancière's unique contribution to the discussion of emancipatory education by showing that, unlike what seems to be the thrust of Freire's view on emancipatory education, there is a clear role, task, and identity for the teacher. Unlike in the case of critical pedagogy this task is not to be understood as that of supplanting false consciousness with true consciousness. But unlike Freire, Rancière doesn't conclude from this that we should do away with the teacher. He rather highlights the problems with the idea that emancipation "runs" on knowledge. This is one sense in which the emancipatory teacher can be called ignorant. The emancipatory teacher is also ignorant because this teacher does not start from knowledge about the alleged incapacity of the student, but rather from the assumption of the equality of intelligence which, as I have shown, is precisely not a matter of knowledge or truth (and here again Rancière takes an approach that is fundamentally different from Freire's).

This, as I have tried to argue, has nothing to do with one way in which Rancière's work has been taken up, which is in terms of the idea that everything in education depends on student meaning-making, and that teachers can only be facilitators of this process but have nothing to give or nothing to add. We should therefore not be fooled by the figure of the ignorant schoolmaster by assuming that schoolmasters who have no knowledge to give also have no teaching to do and should therefore move to the side of the classroom to become facilitators of learning. For Rancière the emancipatory schoolmaster is precisely that: a school-master involved in the act of teaching. And similarly we should not be fooled by the idea that the freedom to learn and, more specifically, the freedom of interpretation and signification, is the way in which we inscribe ourselves in the political project of equality as grown-up subjects, *in* the world but not in the centre of it.

Notes

1 For a similar "problem" in Rancière's engagement with the work of Althusser see Lewis (2012, p. 31). There are also problems with Rancière's conception of learning (see Hallward 2005; Citton 2010). A discussion of this aspect of Rancière's work lies beyond the scope of this chapter.
2 In this and the following section I summarise a main line of thought developed in more detail in Biesta (2010b, 2014).
3 In German: "Der Mensch kann nur Mensch werden durch Erziehung. Er ist nichts, als was die Erziehung aus ihm macht" (Kant 1982, p. 701).
4 In his nuanced reading of Freire, Lewis (2012) seems to underplay this particular aspect of Freire's work and keeps him closer to the neo-Marxist understanding of oppression as the exertion of unwarranted power by the oppressor(s) over the oppressed so that the main emancipatory "act" is that of demystification (see e.g. Lewis 2012, p. 104). Although, as I argue in this chapter, demystification does play a role in Freire's overall conception of emancipatory education, the basic logic of emancipation is conceived in terms of overcoming alienation, not oppressive power.
5 It could be argued that this is exactly where Rancière has fewer qualms – see below.
6 Although here Freire comes closer to the idea of false consciousness, and thus to an understanding of oppression that is closer to neo-Marxist critical theory, his "solution" at this point is not to revert to explanation, but rather to joint action (co-intending, in Freire's vocabulary).
7 This is an important point, because many readers of *The Ignorant Schoolmaster* seem to assume that Rancière simply provides a description of Jacotot's theory and simply endorses this theory. While it is sometimes difficult to see where Jacotot ends and Rancière begins, I nonetheless wish to make a radical distinction between the two and wish to suggest a reading of *The Ignorant Schoolmaster* that focuses on the argument Rancière makes "through" the story of Jacotot. It is of course legitimate to refer to Jacotot's ideas themselves, but in that case I would argue that *The Ignorant Schoolmaster* is an unreliable source for this and readers should rather engage with Jacotot's own writings.
8 To refer to this as an act of revelation is slightly misleading, as it may reduce Rancière's emancipatory logic to that of explanation. Below I provide a different and in my view more accurate formulation of emancipatory teaching, one where the act of emancipatory teaching appears as that of forbidding the student the apparent satisfaction of claiming that one is unable to learn and know without the help of a teacher-explicator.
9 In comparing Freire and Rancière, Lewis (2012) suggests that in Freire we find a focus on freedom with little attention to the question of equality, whereas in Rancière, we find a focus on equality with little attention to the question of freedom. Although it is true that Rancière seeks to articulate a logic of emancipation that starts from the assumption of equality rather than the assumption of inequality, Rancière's observation that students cannot escape the exercise of their liberty indicates that Lewis's claim that "universal teaching remains silent on the question of freedom" (Lewis 2012, p. 73) is perhaps not entirely accurate. After all, as I discuss below, central to the emancipatory "act" of the teacher is the interruption of the students' denial or rejection of their freedom.
10 For a further discussion of differences and similarities between Freire and Rancière see Galloway (2012); see also Lewis (2012).

11 Both formulations sound in a sense remarkably Kantian, as one could imagine that one way in which the emancipatory teacher might enact this is by telling students that they should have the courage to use their own intelligence, which is in line with Kant's formulation of the "motto" of Enlightenment as *Sapere aude!* – have the courage to use your own understanding. On the dimension of encouragement see also Sonderegger (2014). While I agree therefore with Lewis that there is a strong Kantian "streak" in Rancière's work, I would not locate this in the alleged centrality of the emancipatory teacher's "command" to the students that they should follow their own path (see Lewis 2012, pp. 78–79), but in the interruption of the student's denial of their ability to use their own understanding, that is, a denial of their freedom. The difference here has to do with the fact that, as I have suggested in chapter 1, existing as subject is not about just following any path, but is about trying to follow a "grown-up" path, so to speak.

12 In terms of the "uptake" of Rancière's work in the field of education it is probably also important to mention that his argument may not be first and foremost directed at a particular configuration of the school, but that it is first and foremost a critique of society insofar as it operates on a particular logic of schooling – a thesis discussed in more detail in Bingham and Biesta (2010), particularly the concluding chapter "The World Is Not a School".

13 See also chapter 1 in Lewis (2012), which provides a compelling account of the differences and similarities between Rancière and Althusser.

14 The question of educational emancipation must be distinguished from the question of emancipation in the context of art. After all, we should not automatically assume that art is educational, nor that education is "artistic" (on this relationship see also Biesta 2017). I use the word "artistic" in order to distinguish the argument here from the discussion about the aesthetics of education, about which Lewis (2012) has provided a highly original and to a large degree compelling argument. The reason for raising the issue of the relationship between art and education in my argument is because Rancière himself draws the two closely together in *The Emancipated Spectator*.

5

ASKING THE IMPOSSIBLE: TEACHING AS DISSENSUS

In chapter 1 I gave a rather precise formulation of what I believe to be "at stake" in education. I did this by suggesting that the educational task is concerned with arousing the desire in another human being for wanting to exist in and with the world in a grown-up way, that is, as subject. Existing in the world in this way, trying to exist in the world in this way, means that the question of whether what we desire is what we should be desiring has become a living question, a question we carry with us wherever we go, a question we bring into play in whatever we encounter. I have indicated that looking at education in this way is not to be seen as the articulation of a particular preference for what education should aim for, because, as preference, it could always also be otherwise. By referring to it as a task – an *Aufgabe*, something that is *given* to us; an *opdracht*, something we are asked to *carry* – I have tried to indicate that this is not so much a matter of choice as it is something that comes to us when we encounter the "fact of natality" (Arendt 1958, p. 247): the child being born in our midst or the student arriving in our classroom.

Surely, although children are never asked whether they want to be born or not, the desire for life is seldom absent in the newborn child, so that in this regard one might ask whether arousal is needed at all (or whether it is only needed in "extreme" cases). Yet it is important to bear in mind that the desire for life is first of all a desire for *survival*, whereas the desire for wanting to exist in the world in a grown-up way, as subject, refers to a particular way of existing, of *living* one's life, so to speak. Arousing the desire for wanting to live one's life *as subject* means, on the one hand, that we should help children and young people not to overshoot in their ambition to want to be in the world and, on the other hand, that we should help them not to walk away too quickly when they encounter the frustration of the world. With schools this may already be a bit more complicated, as at some point students are likely to realise that they have not been asked whether they want to be there or not (and some may actually raise the same question about their life more generally). This helps to explain why the educational work of teachers, the work that seeks to help students to stay in the difficult middle ground, is indeed difficult work and work that carries risks.

Existing in and with the world as subject means coming to terms with the fact that the world, natural and social, is not a construction or projection of our phantasy, but exists in its own right and its own integrity. To exist as subject, in and with the world, thus means trying to come into dialogue with the world, where dialogue is not to be understood as conversation but as what I have called an existential form. In chapters 2, 3, and 4 I explored this being-in-dialogue in more detail, disentangling our existence as subject from the logic of learning-as-comprehension (chapter 2) and the alleged freedom of signification (chapter 3), working towards the idea that our grown-up subject-ness emerges as a response to an address, a being-spoken-to. This is a moment where *my* subject-ness is "at stake", where I encounter freedom as the very thing that only *I* can do (Levinas) and no one can do in my place. This can be seen as an encounter with the experience of "being taught" or, in a shorter formula, as an encounter with teaching. It is along these lines, as I have suggested in chapter 4, that teaching has emancipatory potential, because it interrupts and potentially liberates us from our being-with-ourselves and calls forth our being-in-the-world-as-subject.

In this chapter I wish to look one more time at teaching, less so in terms of the general work of the teacher and more so in terms of what we might call the *act* of teaching. In contrast to conceptions of teaching that tie it closely to a temporal logic – for example notions of teaching as fostering development or growth or instilling certain capacities or competencies for "later" – I will suggest that when teaching has an interest in and orientation towards the subject-ness of another human being, it operates in an altogether different way. Inspired by Rancière I will refer to this "quality" of teaching as *dissensus*. Dissensus is not to be understood as the absence of consensus or as a moment of disagreement or conflict, but as the introduction of what we might call an "incommensurable element" into an existing state of affairs or, with a phrase from Rancière, a particular "distribution of the sensible". Dissensus, as Rancière explains, is therefore not the "opposition of interests or opinions [but] the production, within a determined, sensible world, of a given that is heterogeneous to it" (Rancière 2003, p. 226).

Dissensus occurs in education when we approach a child or student as subject *precisely* when this flies in the face of all available evidence, that is, of everything that can be seen and known. Yet, as I will discuss in more detail in this chapter, it is precisely this gesture – a teacherly gesture – that opens up a possibility for the child or student to appear as subject. Teaching as dissensus can therefore be seen as a way of asking the impossible from the child or student if, that is, we do not think of the impossible as what is *not* possible but rather conceive of it, following Derrida (1992b, p. 16), as that which cannot be *foreseen* as a possibility, cannot be calculated or predicted from the here and now. Teaching as dissensus, aimed at grown-up subject-ness is precisely characterised by such an orientation towards the unforeseen (see also Torgersen 2015), that is, to what is *not* present, to what can be the object of hope and thus requires faith, but can never be a matter of knowledge or certainty (see Halpin 2003; see also Biesta 2006, chapter 1).

The idea of teaching as dissensus introduces a "logic" that, as mentioned, is quite different from conceptions of teaching that tie it to the child's development or the student's growth. The idea of teaching as dissensus can be said to interrupt such a logic, and therefore raises questions about (our understanding of) the role of time in education. It is here that I would like to start the line of thought I seek to explore in this chapter, for which I want to go back to a short text I published in 2011 together with Carl Anders Säfström which, optimistically, we called *A Manifesto for Education* (see Biesta & Säfström 2011).

Education in the Tension between "What Is" and "What Is Not"

In the *Manifesto* we sought to respond to a number of issues in educational practice, policy, and research. The main discursive device we used in the *Manifesto* was to position what is educational about education – something to which in the *Manifesto* we referred as freedom but which, in the context of this book, can now be described more precisely as grown-up subject-ness – as being "beyond" two options which, in different guises, tend to appear in discussions about education as each other's opposite. In the *Manifesto* we referred to these two options as *populism* and *idealism*.

Populism, so we argued, "shows itself through the simplification of educational concerns by either reducing them to matters of individual taste or to matters of instrumental choice" (Biesta & Säfström 2011, p. 540). It shows itself "through a depiction of educational processes as simple, one-dimensional and straightforward, to be managed by teachers through the ordering of knowledge and the ordering of students, based on scientific evidence about 'what works'" (p. 540). Idealism, on the other hand, "shows itself through overbearing expectations about what education should achieve" (p. 540). Here education "is linked up with projects such as democracy, solidarity, inclusion, tolerance, social justice and peace, even in societies marked by deep social conflict or war" (p. 540). As education never seems to be able to live up to expectations that come either from the side of populism or from the side of idealism, it is constantly being manoeuvred into a position of defence. Whereas:

> some try to counter populism with idealism, arguing that the solution lies in getting the agenda for education 'right,' [others] counter idealism with populism, arguing that with better scientific evidence and better techniques we will eventually be able to fix education and make it work. (Biesta & Säfström 2011, p. 540)

The opposition between populism and idealism can be read as a particular manifestation of a more general opposition between education orientated towards "what is" and education orientated towards "what is not". Both orientations, so we argued, pose a threat to the possibility of freedom. Education under the aegis of "what is" becomes a form of *adaptation*:

> This can either be adaptation to the 'what is' of society, in which case education becomes socialisation. Or it can be adaptation to the 'what is' of the individual child or student, thus starting from such 'facts' as the gifted child, the child with ADHD, the student with learning difficulties, and so on. (Biesta & Säfström 2011, p. 541)

In both cases, however, education loses its orientation towards freedom; it loses its interest in an "excess" that announces something new and unforeseen. We argued, however, that the solution for this problem is *not* to put education under the aegis of the "what is not", because in that case we tie up education with utopian dreams. "To keep education away from pure utopia is not a question of pessimism but a matter of not saddling up education with unattainable hopes that defer freedom rather than that they would make it possible in the here and now" (p. 541). We summarised this by saying that:

> To tie education to the 'what is' is to hand over responsibility for education to forces outside of education, whereas to tie education to the 'what is not' is to hand over education to the thin air of an unattainable future. (Biesta & Säfström 2011, p. 541)

Since what matters educationally about education – freedom – runs the risk of disappearing when we tie education either to "what is" or to "what is not", we suggested in the *Manifesto* that the proper "location" for education is in the *tension* between "what is" and "what is not". While the educational tradition is, in a sense, familiar with this tension, the most common reading of this tension is one where the "what is not" is understood in *temporal* terms, that is, as the "what is not *yet*". The "what is not *yet*" is seen as something that, although it is not "yet" here and now, is expected to arrive at some point in the future. This is perhaps most strongly visible in the way in which the idea of freedom itself figures in modern educational discourse, namely as something that is supposed to arrive at the end of education when the child has learned enough – or in other discourses: has grown enough, has developed enough – so as to be able to take responsibility for its own actions and thus has reached a state of emancipation.

Yet the problem with conceiving of the "what is not" in terms of the "what is not *yet*" and thus seeing education as a process that will deliver its promises at some point in the future, is that the question of freedom disappears from the here and now and thus "runs the risk of being *forever* deferred", as we put it (see

Biesta & Säfström 2011, p. 540; emphasis in original). If it is the case that freedom expresses that which is properly educational about education, then this man-oeuvre runs the risk of locating the educational structurally in a place beyond reach, as always to come but never fully there or, to be more precise: as never fully *here*. The question this raises is whether a temporal understanding of education, one where education is basically seen in terms of some kind of devel-opment over time, can fully capture education's interest in freedom, or whether we should think differently about time and education. This is indeed what we hinted at when we considered the possibility of an educational logic that, unlike the temporal logic of modern education, is explicitly *non*-temporal. It is what we had in mind when we said that education needs to stay in the tension between "what is" and "what is not", and not in the tension between "what is" and "what is not *yet*", and it is this tension to which we referred, after Rancière, as *dissensus*.

To grasp what teaching as dissensus looks like and why and how it matters, I first wish to say a few things about the way in which time plays a role in common understandings of education. I will do this through a brief discussion of six "temporal" concepts that figure in educational discussions: change, learning, development, schooling, the child, and progress.

The Time of Education

Many would indeed argue that *change* is the core "business" of education, both the education of children and the education of adults. After all, if education does not result in any change, one might well say that education has failed or hasn't happened – albeit some changes may take a long time to become visible or take effect. The "act" of education can thus be seen as supporting change, promoting change, facilitating change, even an act of forcing change. And such change is almost always understood in terms of processes that literally take time. Change, after all, is a shift from one state of affairs to another, and thus assumes a certain trajectory in order to get from A to B. In education such trajectories come with value judgements, that is, judgements about the desirability of change. This is why education can be said to have a teleological structure in that it has an orientation towards some desirable "outcome" (which leaves open the question as to who can or should define this outcome and who can or should "desire" this outcome, and also the question as to what extent the "outcome" is or should be fully definable).

From change we can easily move to *learning*, because learning can be seen as a particular form of change – and perhaps it is the form that is generally favoured by educators and educationalists. On the basic but nonetheless widely accepted definition of learning as any more or less permanent change (further specified, for example, as change in cognition, or understanding, or mastery, or skill) that is not the result of maturation, we can argue that what has been said about change can also be said about learning, in that when we have learned something we have changed, and that the process that has led to this change is understood as a learning process. Thus we get definitions of education as supporting, promoting, facilitating, or forcing learning, where learning is seen as a process that takes time. Learning is a process that gets the learner from a particular state of affairs to another state of affairs where the learner has learned something and, in most but not all cases, *realises* that he or she has learned something.

A third concept that plays a central role in education is that of *development.* While development may be seen as a psychological concept – and in a sense it is just that – it continues to structure educational thought and practice, perhaps from Schleiermacher onwards, who saw education as the response of society to the fact of human development, via Piaget and Vygotskij, who both conceived of education as the promotion of development (albeit with different views about the "logic" of this process), via Kohlberg's views on the promotion of the develop-ment of moral reasoning, straight into neuroscience and its claims about the educational promotion of the development of the brain and its functions. Development is perhaps the temporal notion *par excellence* as it carries with it notions of temporal unfolding (in teleological readings of development) or growth-over-time (in non-teleological notions of development). Perhaps we could even say that developmental arguments have had the greatest influence on the temporal construction of education, through the idea either that education needs to *follow* development (which is one way in which Piaget's work has been taken up) or that education can, to a certain degree, *lead or promote* development (which is one way in which Vygotskij's work has been taken up). While pragmatism, particularly through Dewey, criticised a teleological notion of development and replaced it with the notion of "growth", it did keep the temporal structure of education in place, not only by arguing, as Dewey did, that the problem of education lies in achieving co-ordination between individual and social factors – a process that obviously takes time – but even more so by understanding education as the transformation of experience – a thoroughly temporal process.

Perhaps it is important at this point to mention that the conception of time that we can find in the notions of change, learning, and development is a *linear* conception of time, not a *cyclical* one. One could even say that the ideas of change, learning, and development only make sense within the confines of a linear conception of time, so that to understand education in terms of change, learning, and development only became possible with the advance of a linear conception of time itself – an advance that is generally seen as belonging to the rise of a modern worldview and modern society. It is this conception of time that gave rise to the modern idea of what Mollenhauer (1986) refers to as educational time (*Bildungszeit*) (for this see Schaffar 2009, pp. 137–140). Mollenhauer emphasises that the newly developed possibility to provide an exact measurement of time not only resulted in a whole new conception of time, but also led to a temporalisation of life and an economisation of time, the latter being exemplified in the idea that "time is money". The new conception of time and the new temporalisation of life had a profound impact on the organisation of schooling, with regard to both the structure and the content of schooling.

Here Mollenhauer points at the remarkable fact that within a few decennia all over Europe schooling became organised in terms of a particular temporal logic in which education became understood as a linear advance in time, that is as "progressus" or "progressio" (see Mollenhauer 1986, p. 80). In order for this to be possible, education had to be organised in homogeneous groups of children with roughly the same level of development which, in turn, required that the content of education had to be divided up into small temporal units, so that progress in learning would become possible and could be assessed. Hence the need for timetables and curricula (understood as temporal trajectories for progression), and hence the rise of a more general concern for the linear advance of the educational process, ideally without interruption (see Mollenhauer 1986, p. 80). It is also interesting to see that the aims and ends of education became themselves increasingly defined in terms of time rather than with reference to particular achievements. The school day is over, for example, when time is up, not when learning has finished. Compulsory schooling ends at a certain age, not when a particular level of achievement is reached. It is time, therefore, that structures the educational process, rather than that the process has control over the time it needs (see Mollenhauer 1986, p. 80).

If the modern construction of schooling shows us how a particular notion of temporality became the organising principle of the *environment* for education, the conception of the *child* that emerged at the same time shows how this notion of temporality moved to the very centre of our understanding of the child, both in a general sense and more specifically in our conception of the child as an educable being (captured in the German notion of "Bildsamkeit"). The child – the modern child – is understood as a "not-yet", as "in development" and as "in need of education" first and foremost in order to support or promote this development. This is perhaps expressed most poignantly, at least at first sight, in Kant's dictum that the human being can only become human through education. The "not-yet-ness" of the child, the fact that the child needs time in order to become and in order to arrive, not only functions as an argument why education is necessary but also functions as a justification for education. One could say, therefore, that it is not only this child that needs education; it is also education that needs this particular child. When we move from the level of "pedagogics" ("Pädagogik") to that of didactics, we can find a similar way of thinking in the notion of the learner (see also Biesta 2010c), as the learner is precisely defined as the one who is not yet there, the one who lacks something, who is in need of education, and who needs the teacher to fill this lack – either directly through instruction or indirectly by being given tasks that will result in the learning that will fill the lack. And again we can say that just as much as this learner needs teaching, it also teaching that needs this particular learner.

It is perhaps not too far-fetched to note that the temporal construction of the child – and for that matter the temporal construction of the learner – exemplifies a colonial way of thinking in which the other (the child, the learner) is defined as lacking and as "being-in-need-of", *so that* the educator can be in a position to fill the lack and meet the need. While this obviously raises questions of power – questions that are, of course, not unfamiliar to the educational tradition – what I wish to highlight here is the way in which time figures in this colonial relationship. Johannes Fabian, in his book *Time and the Other* (Fabian 1983), has coined the notion of "allochronism" to refer to the way in which modern anthropology constructs its object precisely by denying the simultaneous existence of anthropologists and their objects of study, so that their objects of study become placed in another time. The modern conception of the child as "not-yet" and "in-need-of" works in a similar way by separating the time of the child from the time of the educator, so that education, understood as the activity that bridges the temporal gap, becomes necessary and justified in one and the same move. Schaffar (2009, pp. 107–108) correctly argues, in my view, that what we are encountering here are not empirical facts but rather moral or, as I prefer to call them, normative standpoints. The particular, that is, temporal construction of the child is, therefore, not an empirical phenomenon – which is not to say that empirical facts do not matter – but first and foremost a normative and therefore an educational and a political choice.

The final concept I wish to add to the list is the idea of *progress*, that is, the idea that education is an instrument for progress: the progress of the child, the progress of the community, the progress of the nation, and even the progress of humanity as a whole. Progress, so we might say, structures the entire educational project in terms of a temporal logic in which the future is supposed to be better than the present and in which education is the mediating instrument to bring this better future about. What counts as "better" has a number of different dimensions. Some of them are material – such as the often-heard promise that education is the motor of the knowledge economy that will deliver competitive advantage in the global playing field, or the idea that education is an investment in one's future individual earning power. Others are slightly less materialistic or are indirectly materialistic, such as the idea of education as an investment in one's social and cultural capital, often on the assumption that such capitals can be "cashed in" at a later date. And finally we find educational progress understood in terms of the trajectory towards equality, emancipation, and freedom.

What this brief exploration shows is how pervasive time – and more specifically a linear conception of time – is in the vocabulary of education we appear to be most familiar with and in the ways in which educational processes and practices are being understood, enacted, theorised, and researched. While there is much more to say about each of the concepts and about their history and their politics, my exploration is first and foremost meant to indicate the challenge we face when we try to see whether it is possible to engage differently with the question of time in education or, to be more precise, when we try to take time out of the educational equation. But why would we want to do that?

Teaching beyond Competence

Perhaps a good way to state what is at stake in the ambition to think and do education "beyond" a linear conception of time and think and do teaching *as* dissensus is through an exploration of the idea of competence, as one could argue that the six concepts discussed in the previous section all rely on the idea that education is a process through which children and young people become *more competent*. In developing in a certain direction, in acquiring knowledge and skills through learning, in getting structured support from a schooling system that tries to fit closely with their learning and development, children begin to change, they begin to fill the very lack that defines them, and, if all this is successful, they progress in the desired direction, ending up more knowledgeable, more skilful, and more competent. Education so conceived seems to require that teaching facilitates, supports, directs a little, goes with the flow, so that children and young people progress in the desired direction: teaching as concurrence, rather than teaching as dissensus.

Now all this makes perfect sense as long as education operates in the modes of qualification and socialisation, where we might say that the student is more like an object that acquires knowledge, skills, and ways of doing, and thus becomes a more competent object, but never a subject. Of course, students have to participate in this process and in this regard they are not passive, but even as "active learners", to use a fashionable phrase, they are not a subject. What I am trying to say is that the whole temporal logic of education doesn't "touch" the subject–ness of the student, as this subject–ness is "located" somewhere else. There is of course a whole tradition that sees subject–ness in terms of competence and as competence, where the educational task is seen as that of providing students with the skills of critique and empathy, to name but two, in order to empower their agency. Yet what I have tried to say in the previous chapters is that our subject–ness is not a possession, is not something the self can possess, but that it is an event, something that may or may not occur. It is interesting that when Levinas writes about our subject–ness as "the very fracturing of immanence" (Levinas 1989, p. 204), he actually highlights that this is *not* about our competence, ability, or capacity – "a traumatic upheaval in experience, which confronts intelligence with something far beyond its capacity" (p. 205) – but about "the possibility of a command, a 'you must,' which takes no account of what 'you can'" (p. 205).

Even with all the competences in the world, there is never a guarantee that when the moment comes, when the address arrives, *I* will be there – or, in a formulation that is perhaps slightly clearer albeit less ideal: I will be *able* to be there. Rather than *empowerment*, rather than building up the self with everything that makes the self competent, what we may need instead in order for the address to "come through" and for the subject to "arrive" is *disarmament*, as Jan Masschelein (1997) has convincingly argued. Viewed in this way, the arrival of subject-ness is precisely not the outcome of a developmental trajectory, is not the culmination of a learning trajectory, but an event that breaks through all this, irrespective of whether the child – or anyone of any age, for that matter – is ready for it or not.

This begins to shed light on the claim made in the *Manifesto* that if we think of the child's freedom as that which is not *yet*, if we think of it as something that is supposed to arrive at the end of a successful, empowering, and emancipatory educational trajectory, there is the risk that it may never arrive, that it disappears from the here and now and "runs the risk of being *forever* deferred" (Biesta & Säfström 2011, p. 540; emphasis in original). It is also where Rancière's observations about teaching and emancipation fall in their place, because what Rancière's emancipatory schoolmaster is *not* doing is bringing competence to the student, if that phrase makes sense. He is rather refusing any claim to *in*competence, to the "I am not yet ready", the "I am not yet able", the "I am not yet competent" – and perhaps also to the "I do not want to be a subject yet" or the "I rather prefer to be an object". This is also, then, why *being* emancipated is not a matter of revealing a particular capacity, but about using one's intelligence under the assumption of equality and, through this, inscribing oneself in the political project of equality, as I have put it in chapter 4.

That teaching appears here as dissensus rather than concurrence is first of all because it breaks through the existing state of affairs by refusing the recourse to incapacity and incompetence. In that sense we can already say that teaching as dissensus brings in an incommensurable element into the existing state of affairs, the existing distribution of the sensible, because it refuses to accept the "sense" it finds. But there is a more positive dimension in Rancière's line of thought too, as the refusal to accept incompetence and inequality is at the same time a *verification* of the assumption of the equality of intelligence. Verification, as I have shown in chapter 4, is not to be understood as a matter of proving the truth of this assumption – at stake is not whether it is true or not, which would put every-thing back to the question of competence – but is literally a matter of *making true* (*facere* and *veritas*), that is, *seeing what can be done* if we start from this assumption. The counterfactual nature of the assumption of the equality of intelligence is important here, because the question at stake is not whether this assumption is true, either for this particular case or for all human beings, but is about what may happen if we start from this assumption. Whether it turns out to be true is a question we can only answer in the future, but in order to open up this future as a possible future, we need to act on the assumption that it may be true because only then may we find out whether it is true.

What we encounter here is a rather fundamental educational logic, particularly in relation to the question of subject-ness. One way to grasp what is at stake here, and why this logic is crucially *educational*, is by looking at the role that trust plays in educational relationships and in human relationships more generally. As I have discussed elsewhere in more detail (Biesta 2006, chapter 1), what is interesting about trust is that it is only needed in those situations where we have no secure knowledge about how another human being will act. If we can already predict what another human being will do, there is no point in giving trust and also no need for it; the interaction is purely a matter of calculation, which, in itself, can be fine. Trust comes into play when such a calculation is not possible, and we might of course say that we can never be *entirely* sure how another human being will act or react. From the side of the trust-giver, trust therefore always entails a risk, particularly the risk that the other person will act differently from what we expected or hoped for. Rather than attempting to capture this in moral terms, for example by saying that human beings are fundamentally unreliable, the risk that comes with trust is better to be seen as an acknowledgement of human freedom: the freedom we all have to act in this way or that, to say yes or no, to go with the flow or against it. To trust another human being, to *give trust* to another human being, thus brings this freedom into play. Whether another human being can be trusted, whether he or she "is trustworthy", as it's often put, is the very thing we can only discover when we *give trust*, and when we take the risk involved in giving trust.[1]

It is important to see that the freedom of the one we give trust to is not just realised when the other person does what I hoped for. After all, the possibility not to do so is part of the other's freedom as well, and the other person may well have good reasons for not doing what I hoped for (which we need to distinguish from "just" being unreliable or "just" being untrustworthy). The point is that all these possibilities only become real when trust is given, when we bring in this incommensurable element, something that is not based on any knowledge or evidence and may even go against all the knowledge and evidence we currently have. What is important from an educational point of view is that trust precisely opens up a "space" where the child or student encounters its freedom and where they need to figure out what to do with this freedom. Trust, in other words, puts their subject-ness *at stake*. Without trust, without giving trust, this space may not open and perhaps it is even so that without trust such a space will *never* open, so that the possible *future-as-subject* remains blocked. That is why, with regard to the matter of the child's or student's subject-ness, teaching needs to operate as dissensus; it needs to ask the impossible from the child or student, that is, the very thing that cannot be *foreseen*, predicted, or calculated as a possibility.

This also shows what the problem is with knowing or wanting to know too much about our students and more generally about the ones we encounter in educational relationships, as such knowledge may begin to block the future and, more specifically, their future as subject. This is the problem with too much diagnostic knowledge in education – the idea that we first need to figure out what "the problem" is before we can start acting – and even with the desire to really want to know our students, on the assumption that if we know our students better we can serve them better. This all may be true and may make sense as long as we think in terms of competence and see our task as teacher as that of adding to or growing the competence of our students. But where it concerns their subject-ness the opposite may be the case. Knowing our students too well may not only block them from futures that cannot be foreseen as possibilities from the here and now. It also may block us, as teachers, as educators, from opening up such futures, from trusting that the unforeseen is the very thing that may happen. When we do not know who our students are, when we do not know where they have come from, when we do not have knowledge of all their baggage, we may precisely be able to approach them in new and unimagined ways that also release them from the burden of their past, their history, their problems, and their diagnoses.

The problem with fixing our educational endeavours too tightly to the presumed competence of our students becomes even more of an "issue" in those cases where competence can be said to be lacking, something that is at stake in the domain usually referred to as "special education" (though from what I am trying to do in this chapter one may wonder how "special" special education actually is). In a paper focusing on educators working with "youth labelled as autistic" (Hudak 2011, p. 58), Glen Hudak makes the point that if one were to base one's educational endeavours squarely on this "label", this diagnosis, education would only be able to repeat what allegedly is already "there", and would end up tying education and the one being educated to their "what is". Hudak, however, argues for the opposite case, suggesting that the very possibility for education only opens up when the educator acts on the basis of three presumptions: the presumption of competence, the presumption of imagination, and the presumption of intimacy (see Hudak 2011, p. 58). And in each case Hudak makes the point that the onus is not on the young person to communicate and relate in an "accepted" manner, so to speak, but on the educator "to figure out how we can help those with physical impairments better communicate their experience, and hence be included into discussions rather than remaining on the sideline, spoken for by others" (p. 61).

Biklen and Cardinal (1997, quoted in Hudak 2011, p. 61) make the point as follows:

> We do not expect readers to believe as a matter of faith that certain people can do things they have not demonstrated themselves capable of doing. [… However,] adopting the conception of 'presuming competence' places an onus of responsibility on educators and researchers to figure out how the person using facilitation, or any educational undertaking, can better demonstrate ability.

The task for the "outsider", therefore, "is not to interpret the world for those labelled autistic [but rather] to presume that the person labelled autistic is a thinking, feeling person" (Hudak 2011, p. 61). Hudak makes similar points in relation to the other two presumptions – those of imagination and intimacy – and with regard to all three presumptions he argues that they pose "at once a philosophical and political challenge" (p. 66), in that they require us not only to fundamentally rethink what it means to speak, communicate, and relate, but, by acting upon these assumptions, also to challenge "dominant structures of power" (p. 66) and dominant definitions "of what it means to be human" (p. 62). And this, as Hudak concludes, is not only relevant "for those labelled 'disabled'" but actually for "all of us" (p. 69), thus showing that what is special about special education may not be that special at all, at least not from the point of view of teaching and the teacher.

Conclusion: Seeing What Is Not Visible; Not Seeing What Is Visible

One could summarise the main thrust of this chapter by saying that teachers ought to have faith in their students. I would be happy with such a summary, particularly if we connect it to the idea of a leap of faith (or a leap to faith, as Kierkegaard would have it), which highlights that to have faith indeed requires a leap rather than that it is a simple logical deduction from what we know. This is indeed the point I have been trying to make, that with regard to the question of the subject-ness of the student, teaching operates as dissensus, as a break with all the evidence in front of us in order to open up a future within which the student can exist as subject. It is, to paraphrase Rancière, acting on the basis of the subject-ness of the student that opens up a future within which the student can appear as subject. If we wait until we have all the evidence that the student is competent enough to be trusted – trusted with their freedom, trusted with their subject-ness – we run the risk of postponing the moment where the student can appear as subject until the end of time, as we may always be looking for more assurances, more details we want to be certain about, and so on.

The leap of faith needs to break through all this by, against all evidence, against all that is visible, approaching the student *as subject*, because it is only by doing so that a situation opens up within which the student may or may not appear as such. This is what it means for teaching to "operate" as dissensus; this is what it means to bring an incommensurable element into the existing state of affairs, the existing distribution of the sensible. To do so means that as teachers we orient our actions towards that which is not visible in the here and now – the student's subject-ness – which is a matter of seeing what is not visible. At the same time, as I have tried to argue in this chapter, it requires that we close our eyes to what is visible, to the "evidence" that tries to tell us that the student is not yet ready, that the student has been unreliable in the past, has abused our trust, and so on. All that may be true, and all that may be taken into consideration, but if we tie the student only to his or her past, only to everything that is known so far, we block the possibility of a different future. That is why there is a limit to what we should want to know about our students and why teaching as dissensus, teaching aimed at our students' subject-ness, teaching that in some strange way seeks to arouse the desire in the student for wanting to exist in the world as subject, should actually not want to know anything at all about the student who arrives in our classroom or, for that matter, the child being born in our midst.

Note

1 Note that the risk is not only the risk that the other person may act differently; in the very same gesture we also put ourselves at risk – particularly in education. See also what I have said in chapter 1 about power, authority, and the risk of teaching.

EPILOGUE: GIVING TEACHING BACK TO EDUCATION

In the foregoing chapters I have tried to make a case for teaching, for the importance of teaching, for the significance of teaching, and even for the need for teaching. I have done so in response to recent developments in the theory, policy, and practice of education – developments that generally have given teaching a bad name. The main bone of contention seems to be the idea that teaching is ultimately a form of control in which students are treated as objects and not as subjects. Given that education, unlike indoctrination, has an interest in the freedom of the student, that is, in their existence as subjects, the conclusion can only be that teaching stands in the way of the realisation of this freedom.

As shown, we can see the impact of this line of thinking in the critique of so-called "traditional" teaching that has led to a development where the teacher has been moved from being a "sage on the stage" – itself already a pejorative depiction – to a "guide on the side" and eventually a "peer at the rear". In the latter position teachers are no longer distinguishable from their students but have morphed into fellow learners who are part of wider learning communities. The critique of teaching as control also plays a role in discussions about emancipatory education. It is one of the main reasons why Freire, in his ambition to overcome the "teacher-student contradiction", ends up with education as the joint praxis of "teacher-student with student-teachers". And it lies behind the claim that neo-Marxist forms of critical pedagogy, despite their good intentions, still do not really "feel empowering", because they still rely on powerful acts of demystification.

Ironically, in those cases where there still seems to be an appetite for teaching, control is also the main theme. Recent claims about the teacher as the most important "factor" in the educational process are, after all, interested in making this "factor" more effective so that the production of learning outcomes becomes more predictable and secure. Teachers who are unable to contribute effectively to this ambition nowadays even run the risk of losing their job, on the assumption that doing the job well would mean being "in control" of this particular production cycle. Similarly the issue of teaching as control is central in calls for restoring the authority of the teacher – and behind that: authority itself – as part of a wider concern about an alleged lack of authority in modern societies (albeit the interest here is more often than not one of power – which is unidirectional – rather than one of authority – which, as mentioned, is always relational).

This then seems to be the dilemma concerning teaching in contemporary educational debates: those who have an interest in teaching are not really interested in the freedom of the student, and those who are interested in the students' freedom see teaching as an impediment to it. This is not just a theoretical problem about the connection between teaching and freedom, although, as I have tried to show in the previous chapters, there are important theoretical issues to be tackled as well. It is not just a political problem about the role and status of teachers in contemporary schooling, although there are important and urgent issues with regard to politics, policy, teaching, and the teacher here too. It is also, and perhaps first and foremost, a problem that goes to the heart of what it means to be a teacher and even what it means to exist as a teacher. After all, it seems that those who believe in education are forced to move themselves to the back of the classroom where they end up as fellow-learners, unable any longer to articulate what their unique responsibility is. Whereas those who want to stay in front of the classroom because they believe that that is their proper place and the position from which they can make sense of their unique responsibility as teacher are being told that they do not really believe in education, that they are "out of date". Or to put it (a bit too) bluntly: if you want to be progressive you can't really want to be a teacher, whereas if you want to be a teacher it can only mean that you must be (a) conservative.

Before we accept this conclusion – and I see many instances in many countries where these seem to be the only two options "on the table" – I think that it is important to consider the possibility of the third option, one where teaching has an important and perhaps even essential role to play in education interested in and orientated towards the freedom of the student. Such a "progressive argument for a conservative idea" is intended *to give teaching back to education*, as I have put it in one of my previous publications (Biesta 2012b) and also in the title of this epilogue; an ambition which, interestingly, I have seen being re-presented a number of times as the ambition to give education back to the teacher, which may be important as well but, from my perspective, is an entirely different matter and an entirely different ambition. To search for a third option, reconnecting teaching to the question of human freedom, is what I have been trying to do in the previous chapters.

One important building block of this endeavour concerns the question of freedom, which explains why this question plays such a prominent role in the discussion and why it returns, in different guises, throughout the book. Against the idea of what we might call neo-liberal freedom, that is, the idea of freedom as pure choice or, in less philosophical language, the freedom of shopping, the freedom just to pursue your desires, I have tried to make a case for grown-up freedom. Grown-up freedom is not the sovereign freedom Hannah Arendt has rightly criticised, but freedom-as-action (Arendt), the "difficult freedom" (Levinas 1990) we encounter when we try to exist in and with the world and not just with ourselves. There we "meet" the question of whether what we desire, the desires we find "in" ourselves, are the desires that will help us to exist in and with the world in a grown-up way – in the world, without being in the centre of the world (Meirieu). That is what it means to exist as subject, not object, in the difficult "middle ground".

The theme of learning, which plays a prominent role in chapters 2 and 3, is connected to the question of freedom as well, not in order to do away with learning but to show that learning is only one existential possibility, only one way to exist, and that there may be other existential possibilities that we should consider in our lives and hence should encounter in educational settings. I have also, following Levinas, questioned the alleged "freedom of signification" – which is a way to understand what learning is about; an act of sense-making, under-standing, comprehension – and have suggested, with Levinas, that signification is always secondary to interlocution, as Levinas puts it: that the address, the being spoken to, comes before the sense-making.

Teaching, from this angle, is then no longer a matter of creating a space where students can *be free* – for example, can be free to learn, can be free to make sense, can be free to comprehend – but is about creating a space, to use the spatial metaphor for a moment (on this see also chapter 5 in Biesta 2006; and Biesta in press), where students can *encounter their freedom*, can encounter the very thing that "nobody else can do in my place", to refer to Levinas one more time. That is why teaching, if it is aimed at grown-up freedom, at the existence of the student as subject, not object, "operates" as dissensus – not (just) building up their capacities and capabilities but turning students towards their freedom, towards this impos-sible possibility (Derrida), the possibility that cannot be *foreseen* as a possibility, of existing in the world as subject.

Is this enough for the recovery of teaching and the rediscovery of its meaning and significance? Is this enough for reconnecting teaching with the progressive ambitions of education? Is this enough for giving teaching back to education? Probably not. But I do hope that my explorations will help in getting a better sense of what the issues concerning the status of teaching and the teacher in con-temporary education are. I also hope that my explorations will inspire others in the search for the third option, beyond teaching as control and freedom as learning. And I hope that my explorations will provide some support to those who believe that teaching matters, not for the effective production of learning outcomes, but for our existence as grown-up subjects, in the world but not in the centre of it.

ABOUT THE AUTHOR

At the time of writing this book, **Gert J. J. Biesta** (www.gertbiesta.com) is Professor of Education and Director of Research in the Department of Education of Brunel University London, UK (0.8), and NIVOZ Professor for Education at the University of Humanistic Studies, the Netherlands (0.2). In addition, he is Professor II at NLA University College Bergen, Norway. In 2015 he was invited to join the Education Council of the Netherlands, which is the advisory body of the Dutch government and parliament on educational matters. Gert Biesta has published extensively on the theory and philosophy of education and the theory and philosophy of educational and social research and has reported on his work in many books, articles, and chapters that, so far, have appeared in sixteen different languages. From 1999 until 2014 he was editor-in-chief of the journal *Studies in Philosophy and Education*. In 2016 he became an associate editor of *Educational Theory*. In 2011–2012 he served as President of the Philosophy of Education Society USA, being the first president from outside North America. Gert Biesta has worked at universities in several countries and has been residing in the UK since 1999, calling Scotland his home since 2007. When not working, Gert Biesta enjoys doing nothing.

REFERENCES

Andreotti, V. (2011). *Actionable postcolonial theory in education*. New York: Palgrave Macmillan.

Arendt, H. (1958). *The human condition*. Chicago, IL: The University of Chicago Press.

Arendt, H. (1977[1961]). *Between past and future: Eight exercises in political thought*. Enlarged edition. Harmondsworth/New York: Penguin Books.

Bauman, Z. (1993). *Postmodern ethics*. Oxford: Wiley-Blackwell.

Biesta, G.J.J. (1999). Radical intersubjectivity. Reflections on the "different" foundation of education. *Studies in Philosophy and Education* 18(4), 203–220.

Biesta, G.J.J. (2004). "Mind the gap!" Communication and the educational relation. In C. Bingham & A.M. Sidorkin (eds), *No education without relation* (pp. 11–22). New York: Peter Lang.

Biesta, G.J.J. (2006). *Beyond learning: Democratic education for a human future*. Boulder, CO: Paradigm Publishers.

Biesta, G.J.J. (2007). Why 'what works' won't work. Evidence-based practice and the democratic deficit of educational research. *Educational Theory* 57(1), 1–22.

Biesta, G.J.J. (2008). Pedagogy with empty hands: Levinas, education and the question of being human. In D. Egéa-Kuehne (ed), *Levinas and education: At the intersection of faith and reason* (pp. 198–210). London/New York: Routledge.

Biesta, G.J.J. (2009a). Good education in an age of measurement: On the need to reconnect with the question of purpose in education. *Educational Assessment, Evaluation and Accountability* 21(1), 33–46.

Biesta, G.J.J. (2009b). Pragmatism's contribution to understanding learning-in-context. In R. Edwards, G.J.J. Biesta & M. Thorpe (eds), *Rethinking contexts for teaching and learning. Communities, activities and networks* (pp. 61–73). London/New York: Routledge.

Biesta, G.J.J. (2009c). What is at stake in a pedagogy of interruption? In T.E. Lewis, J.G.A. Grinberg & M. Laverty (eds), *Philosophy of education: Modern and contemporary ideas at play* (pp. 785–807). Dubuque, IA: Kendall/Hunt.

Biesta, G.J.J. (2010a). *Good education in an age of measurement: Ethics, politics, democracy*. Boulder, CO: Paradigm Publishers.

Biesta, G.J.J. (2010b). A new 'logic' of emancipation: The methodology of Jacques Rancière. *Educational Theory* 60(1), 39–59.

Biesta, G.J.J. (2010c). Learner, student, speaker. Why it matters how we call those we teach. *Educational Philosophy and Theory* 42(4), 540–552.

Biesta, G.J.J. (2010d). How to exist politically and learn from it: Hannah Arendt and the problem of democratic education. *Teachers College Record* 112(2), 558–577.

Biesta, G.J.J. (2011a). The ignorant citizen: Mouffe, Rancière, and the subject of democratic education. *Studies in Philosophy and Education* 30(2), 141–153.

Biesta, G.J.J. (2011b). Disciplines and theory in the academic study of education: A comparative analysis of the Anglo-American and Continental construction of the field. *Pedagogy, Culture and Society* 19(2), 175–192.

Biesta, G.J.J. (2012a). No education without hesitation. Thinking differently about educational relations. In C. Ruitenberg (ed), *Philosophy of education 2012* (pp. 1–13). Urbana-Champaign, IL: PES.

Biesta, G.J.J. (2012b). Giving teaching back to education. Responding to the disappearance of the teacher. *Phenomenology and Practice* 6(2), 35–49.

Biesta, G.J.J. (2013a). Receiving the gift of teaching: From 'learning from' to 'being taught by'. *Studies in Philosophy and Education* 32(5), 449–461.

Biesta, G.J.J. (2013b). Interrupting the politics of learning. *Power and Education* 5(1), 4–15.

Biesta, G.J.J. (2014). *The beautiful risk of education*. Boulder, CO: Paradigm Publishers.

Biesta, G.J.J. (2015). Resisting the seduction of the global education measurement industry: Notes on the social psychology of PISA. *Ethics and Education* 10(3), 348–360.

Biesta, G.J.J. (2016). Democracy and education revisited: Dewey's democratic deficit. In S. Higgins & F. Coffield (eds), *John Dewey's education and democracy: A British tribute* (pp. 149–169). London: IoE Press.

Biesta, G.J.J. (2017). *Letting art teach. Art education 'after' Joseph Beuys*. Arnhem: ArtEZ Press.

Biesta, G.J.J. (in press). Creating spaces for learning or making room for education? The architecture of education revisited. In H.M. Tse, H. Daniels, A. Stables & A. Cox (eds), *Design for practice: Designing for the future of schooling*. London/New York: Routledge.

Biesta, G.J.J. & Bingham, C. (2012). Response to Caroline Pelletier's review of Jacques Rancière: Education, truth, emancipation. *Studies in Philosophy and Education* 31(6), 621–623.

Biesta, G.J.J. & Burbules, N. (2003). *Pragmatism and educational research*. Lanham, MD: Rowman and Littlefield.

Biesta, G.J.J. & Säfström, C.A. (2011). A manifesto for education. *Policy Futures in Education* 9(5), 540–547.

Biklen, D. & Cardinal, D.N. (1997). Reframing the issue: Presuming competence. In D. Biklen & D.N. Cardinal (eds), *Contested words, contested science: Unraveling the facilitated communication controversy* (pp. 187–198). New York: Teachers College Press.

Bingham, C. (2008). *Authority is relational. Rethinking educational empowerment*. Albany, NY: SUNY Press.

Bingham, C. & Biesta, G.J.J. (2010). *Jacques Rancière: Education, truth, emancipation*. London/New York: Continuum.

Carusi, F.T. (in press). Why bother teaching? Despairing the ethical through teaching that does not follow. *Studies in Philosophy and Education*.

Chambers, S.A. (2013). Jacques Rancière's lesson on the lesson. *Educational Philosophy and Theory* 45(6), 637–646.

Citton, Y. (2010). The ignorant schoolmaster: Knowledge and authority. In J.-P. Deranty (ed), *Jacques Rancière: Key concepts* (pp. 25–37). Durham: Acumen.

Cohen, R.A. (2006). Introduction. In E. Levinas, *Humanism of the other* (pp. vii–xliv). Urbana/Chicago: University of Illinois Press.

Counts, G. (1971). A humble autobiography. In R.J. Havighurst (ed), *Leaders of American education: The seventieth yearbook of the National Society for the Study of Education* (pp. 151–171). Chicago, IL: University of Chicago Press.

Critchley, S. (1999). *Ethics, politics, subjectivity*. London/New York: Verso.

Critchley, S. (2014). Levinas and Hitlerism. *Graduate Faculty Philosophy Journal* 35(1–2), 223–249.

Department for Education (2010). *The importance of teaching. The schools white paper 2010*. London: Her Majesty's Stationery Office.

Derrida, J. (1992a). *Given time: I. Counterfeit money*. Trans. P. Kamuf. Chicago/London: University of Chicago Press.

Derrida, J. (1992b). Force of law. The 'mystical foundation of authority'. In D. Cornell, M. Rosenfeld & D.G. Carlson (eds), *Deconstruction and the possibility of justice* (pp. 3–67). New York/London: Routledge.

Derrida, J. (1995). *The gift of death*. Trans. D. Wills. Chicago/London: University of Chicago Press.

Dewey, J. (1925). Experience and nature. In J.A. Boydston (ed), *John Dewey. The later works (1925–1953), Volume 1*. Carbondale/Edwardsville: Southern Illinois University Press.

Dewey, J. (1933). *How we think. A restatement of the relation of reflective thinking to the educative process*. Boston, MA: D.C. Heath and Company.

Dewey, J. (1966[1916]). *Democracy and education*. New York: The Free Press.

Donaldson, G. (2010). *Teaching Scotland's future: Report of a review of teacher education in Scotland*. Edinburgh: Scottish Government.

Drerup, J. (2015). Autonomy, perfectionism and the justification of education. *Studies in Philosophy and Education* 34(1), 63–87.

Eagleton, T. (2007). *Ideology: An introduction*. New and updated edition. London/New York: Verso.

Ellsworth, E. (1989). Why doesn't this feel empowering? Working through the repressive myths of critical pedagogy. *Harvard Educational Review* 59(3), 297–325.

Engels-Schwarzpaul, A.-C. (2015). The ignorant supervisor: About common worlds, epistemological modesty and distributed knowledge. *Educational Philosophy and Theory* 47(12), 1250–1264.

Fabian, J. (1983). *Time and the other. How anthropology makes its object*. New York: Columbia University Press.

Faure, E., Herrera, F., Kaddoura, A.-R., Lopes, H., Petrovsky, A.V., Rahnema, M. & Champion Ward, F. (eds) (1972). *Learning to be. The world of education today and tomorrow*. Paris: UNESCO.

Fenstermacher, G.D. (1986). Philosophy of research on teaching: Three aspects. In M.C. Wittrock (ed), *Handbook of research on teaching*. 3rd edition (pp. 37–49). New York: Macmillan; London: Collier Macmillan.

Field, J. (2000). *Lifelong learning and the new educational order*. Stoke-on-Trent: Trentham.

Freire, P. (1993). *Pedagogy of the oppressed*. New, revised 20th anniversary edition. New York: Continuum.

Galloway, S. (2012). Reconsidering emancipatory education: Staging a conversation between Paulo Freire and Jacques Rancière. *Educational Theory* 62(2), 163–184.

Gordon, P.E. (2012). *Continental divide. Heidegger, Cassirer, Davos*. Cambridge, MA: Harvard University Press.

Hallward, P. (2005). Jacques Rancière and the subversion of mastery. *Paragraph* 28(1), 26–45.

Halpin, D. (2003). *Hope and education: The role of the utopian imagination.* London: Routledge-Falmer.

Heydorn, H.J. (1972). *Zu einer Neufassung des Bildungsbegriffs* [Towards a new articulation of the concept of 'Bildung']. Frankfurt am Main: Suhrkamp.

Hodkinson, P., Biesta, G.J.J. & James, D. (2008). Understanding learning culturally: Overcoming the dualism between social and individual views of learning. *Vocations and Learning* 1(1), 27–47.

Hudak, G. (2011). Alone in the presence of others: Autistic sexuality and intimacy reconsidered. In D. Carlson & D. Roseboro (eds), *The sexuality curriculum and youth culture* (pp. 57–70). New York: Peter Lang.

Ileris, K. (2008). *Contemporary theories of learning.* London: Routledge.

Jaeger, W. (1945). *Paideia: The ideals of Greek culture.* New York: Oxford University Press.

Kant, I. (1982). Über Pädagogik [On education]. In I. Kant, *Schriften zur Anthropologie, Geschichtsphilosophie, Politik und Pädagogik* [Writings on anthropology, the philosophy of history, politics and education] (pp. 691–761). Frankfurt am Main: Insel Verlag.

Kant, I. (1992[1784]). An answer to the question 'What is Enlightenment?' In P. Waugh (ed), *Post-modernism: A reader* (p. 90). London: Edward Arnold.

Klafki, W. (1986). Die Bedeutung der klassischen Bildungstheorien fur eine zeitgemasses Konzept von allgemeiner Bildung [The significance of classical theories of 'Bildung' for a contemporary conception of general 'Bildung']. *Zeitschrift für Pädagogik* 32(4), 455–476.

Klafki, W. & Brockmann, J.-L. (2003). *Geisteswissenschaftliche Pädagogik und Nationalsozialismus. Herman Nohl und seine 'Göttinger Schule', 1932–1937* [Hermeneutic educational theory and national socialism: Herman Nohl and his 'Göttinger Schule']. Weinheim: Beltz.

Kneyber, R. & Evers, J. (eds) (2015). *Flip the system: Changing education from the bottom up.* London: Routledge.

Komisar, P. (1968). Teaching: Act and enterprise. *Studies in Philosophy and Education* 6(2), 168–193.

Lankshear, C. & McLaren, P. (1994). *The politics of liberation: Paths from Freire.* New York: Routledge.

Levinas, E. (1969[1961]). *Totality and infinity: An essay on exteriority.* Pittsburgh, PA/The Hague: Duquesne University Press/Martinus Nijhoff.

Levinas, E. (1985). *Ethics and infinity. Conversations with Philippe Nemo.* Pittsburgh, PA: Duquesne University Press.

Levinas, E. (1989). Revelation in the Jewish tradition. In S. Hand (ed), *The Levinas reader* (pp. 190–211). Oxford: Blackwell.

Levinas, E. (1990[1934]). Reflections on the philosophy of Hitlerism. Translated by S. Hand. *Critical Inquiry* 17(1), 62–71.

Levinas, E. (1990). *Difficult freedom. Essays on Judaism.* Translated by S. Hand. Baltimore, MD: The Johns Hopkins University Press.

Levinas, E. (1994). *Outside the subject.* Stanford, CA: Stanford University Press.

Levinas, E. (2006). *Humanism of the other.* Translated by Nidra Poller, introduction by Richard A. Cohen. Urbana/Chicago: University of Illinois Press.

Levinas, E. (2008). Meaning and sense. In A.T. Peperzak, S. Critchley & R. Bernasconi (eds), *Emmanuel Levinas: Basic philosophical writings* (pp. 33–64). Bloomington, IN: Indiana University Press.

Lewis, T. (2012). *The aesthetics of education. Theatre, curiosity and politics in the work of Jacques Rancière and Paulo Freire.* London/New York: Bloomsbury.

Lingis, A. (1994). *The community of those who have nothing in common*. Bloomington, IN: Indiana University Press.

Løvlie, L. (2002). Rousseau's insight. *Studies in Philosophy and Education* 21(4–5), 335–341.

Luhmann, N. (1984). *Soziale Systeme: Grundriß einer allgemeinen Theorie* [Social systems: Outline of a general theory]. Frankfurt am Main: Suhrkamp.

Luhmann, N. (1995). *Social systems*. Stanford, CA: Stanford University Press.

MacMillan, C.J.B. & Nelson, T. (eds) (1968). *Concepts of teaching*. Chicago, IL: Rand McNally.

Masschelein, J. (1997). In defence of education as problematisation: Some preliminary notes on a strategy of disarmament. In D. Wildemeersch, M. Finger & T. Jansen (eds), *Adult education and social responsibility: Reconciling the irreconcilable?* (pp. 133–149). Frankfurt/Bern: Peter Lang.

Maturana, H.R. & Varela, F.J. (1980). *Autopoiesis and cognition: The realization of the living*. Dordrecht: D. Reidel Publishing Company.

McKinsey & Co. (2007). *McKinsey Report: How the world's best-performing school systems come out on top*. http://mckinseyonsociety.com/downloads/reports/Education/Worlds_School_Systems_Final.pdf (accessed 07/01/15).

McLaren, P. (1997). *Revolutionary multiculturalism: Pedagogies of dissent for the new millennium*. Boulder, CO: Westview Press.

Meirieu, P. (2007). *Pédagogie: Le devoir de resister* [Education: The duty to resist]. Issy-les-Moulineaux: ESF éditeur.

Mollenhauer, K. (1976[1968]). *Erziehung und Emanzipation*. 6th edition [Education and emancipation]. München: Juventa.

Mollenhauer, K. (1986). Zur Entstehung der modernen Konzepts von Bildungszeit [On the emergence of the modern conception of educational time]. In K. Mollenhauer, *Umwege: Über Bildung, Kunst und Interaktion* [Diversions: On education, art and interaction] (pp. 68–92). Weinheim: Juventa.

Noddings, N. (2012). *Philosophy of education*. 3rd edition. Boulder, CO: Westview Press.

OECD (2005). *Teachers matter: Attracting, developing and retaining effective teachers*. Paris: OECD.

Pelletier, C. (2012). Review of Charles Bingham and Gert Biesta, Jacques Rancière: Education, truth, emancipation, Continuum 2010. *Studies in Philosophy and Education* 31(6), 613–619.

Peters, R.S. (1967). What is an educational process? In R.S. Peters (ed), *The concept of education* (pp. 1–23). London: Routledge/Kegan Paul.

Priestley, M., Biesta, G.J.J. & Robinson, S. (2015). *Teacher agency: An ecological approach*. London: Bloomsbury.

Rancière, J. (1991). *The ignorant schoolmaster. Five lessons in intellectual emancipation*. Translated and with an introduction by Kristin Ross. Stanford, CA: Stanford University Press.

Rancière, J. (2003). *The philosopher and his poor*. Durham, NC/London: Duke University Press.

Rancière, J. (2009). *The emancipated spectator*. London: Verso.

Rancière, J. (2010). On ignorant schoolmasters. In C. Bingham & G.J.J. Biesta, *Jacques Rancière: Education, truth, emancipation* (pp. 1–24). London/New York: Continuum.

Rancière, J. (2011). Ebbing the tide. An interview with Jacques Rancière. In P. Bowman & R. Stamp (eds), *Reading Rancière: Critical dissensus* (pp. 238–251). London: Continuum.

Richardson, V. (2003). Constructivist pedagogy. *Teachers College Record* 105(9), 1623–1640.

Roberts, P. (2014). *The impulse society. What is wrong with getting what we want?* London: Bloomsbury.

Rogers, G. (1969). *Freedom to learn. A view of what education might become.* Columbus, OH: Charles E. Merrill.

Roth, W.-M. (2011). *Passability. At the limits of the constructivist metaphor.* Dordrecht/Boston, MA: Springer Science & Business Media.

Ryle, G. (1952). *The concept of mind.* London: Hutchinsons.

Sartre, J.P. (2007[1946]). *Existentialism is a humanism* (translated by C. Macomber, introduction by A. Cohen-Solal, notes and preface by A. Elkaïm-Sartre). New Haven, CT: Yale University Press.

Schaffar, B. (2009). *Allgemeine Pädagogik im Zweispalt: Zwischen epistemologische Neutralität und moralischer Einsicht* [General educational theory at the crossroads: Between epistemological neutrality and moral insight]. Würzburg: Ergon Verlag.

Smeyers, P. & Depaepe, M. (eds) (2006). *Educational research: Why 'what works' doesn't work.* Dordrecht: Springer.

Sonderegger, R. (2014). Do we need others to emancipate ourselves? Remarks on Jacques Rancière. *Krisis. Journal for Contemporary Philosophy* 34(1), 53–67.

Spivak, G. (1988). Can the subaltern speak? In C. Nelson & L. Grossberg (eds), *Marxism and the interpretation of culture* (pp. 271–313). Urbana: University of Illinois Press.

Spivak, G.C. (2004). Righting the wrongs. *South Atlantic Quarterly* 103(2/3), 523–581.

Stamp, R. (2013). Of slumdogs and schoolmasters: Jacotot, Rancière and Mitra on self-organized learning. *Educational Philosophy and Theory* 45(6), 647–662.

Stanley, W.B. (1992). *Curriculum for utopia: Social reconstructionism and critical pedagogy in the postmodern era.* Albany, NY: SUNY Press.

Thompson, A. (1997). What to do while waiting for the revolution. Political pragmatism and performance pedagogy. In S. Laird (ed), *Philosophy of education 1997* (pp. 189–197). Urbana-Champaign, IL: Philosophy of Education Society.

Torgersen, G.-E. (ed) (2015). *Pedagogikk for det uforutsette* [Education for the unforeseen]. Bergen: Fagbokforlaget.

Varela, F.J., Maturana, H.R. & Uribe, R. (1974). Autopoiesis: The organization of living systems, its characterization and a model. *Biosystems* 5(4), 187–196.

von Braunmühl, E. (1975). *Antipädagogik. Studien zur Abschaffung der Erziehung* [Anti-education: Essays on the abolition of education]. Weinheim: Beltz.

Yang, J. & Valdés-Cotera, R. (eds) (2011). *Conceptual evolution and policy developments in lifelong learning.* Hamburg: UNESCO Institute for Lifelong Learning.

Zhao, G. (2014). Freedom reconsidered: Heteronomy, open subjectivity, and the 'gift of teaching'. *Studies in Philosophy and Education* 33(5), 513–525.

Zhao, G. (2015). From the philosophy of consciousness to the philosophy of difference: The subject of education after humanism. *Educational Philosophy and Theory* 47(9), 958–969.

INDEX

Ileris, K. 30
imagination: presumption of 93, 94
immanence 13, 15, 17, 46–8, 52–3, 55, 90
imperialism 51, 52
impossible possibility 98
impulse society 4, 17
incapability 74
incapacity 91
inclusion 84
incommensurable element 6, 83, 92, 94
indoctrination 25
inequality 69, 71, 80n, 91; see also equality
infantilism 16–18
intellectualism 38n; see also constructivism
intelligence 70–1, 73–7, 81n, 90–1:
   intelligence: equality of 79, 91
intelligent adaptive systems 5, 44–7, 55, 56
intelligibility 53–4
intentionality 33
interlocution 49, 50, 52, 98
interpretation 43, 46, 55
interruption 16–20
intervention 62–3
intimacy: presumption of 93, 94
irreplaceability: uniqueness as 11–13

Jacotot, J. 68–71, 75, 77, 80n
Jaeger, W. 60
James, D. 25
joint learning 65; see also co-intentional
   learning

Kant, I. 32, 60, 76, 80n, 81n, 88
Klafki, W. 60, 61
Kneyber, R. 2
knowledge 84: construction 3; education
   and 28; role of 6; transmission of 72, 74,
   76–7
Komisar, P. 24, 25, 27
kritische Pädagogik 61; see also critical
   pedagogy

language and logic of learning 1, 5, 22
language of education 28–9
language of learning 27–9, 32, 44
Lankshear, C. 63
learnification of education 23, 27–9
learning, concept of 24, 35, 37: activity
   25–6; definitions of 25; process 25;
   temporal concept 86–7
learning difficulties 85
learning environments 27, 44–7
learning opportunities 45

learning outcomes 2, 96–7: production of
   23, 98
learning-centred education 1
Levinas, E. 5, 11–13, 15, 16, 17, 21n, 41,
   43–4, 47–59, 83, 90, 98
Lewis, T. 64, 80n, 81n
liberation 9, 60–1, 73: emancipatory
   education 73; from dogmatism 61; see
   also freedom
libertarian pedagogy 66
lifelong learning 2, 27, 29–30, 45: Shanghai
   Forum 29–30
Ligthart, J. 41
Lincoln, A. 41
Lingis, A. 8, 12
listening 34
liturgy: rediscovery of teaching 49–50
Locke, J. 32
love 54
Løvlie, L. 60, 61
Luhmann, N. 46

MacMillan, C.J.B. 25
making sense 10, 33, 36, 57n, 78; see also
   sense-making
Marxism 5, 61–3; see neo-Marxist critical
   pedagogy
Masschelein, J. 91
master-explicator 69–70
materialism 89
Maturana, H.R. 45
McKinsey & Co. 1
McLaren, P. 61, 63
Mead, G. H. 57n
meaning-making 3, 5, 40–1
Meirieu, P. 2, 8–9, 42, 98
middle ground 19; see also self-destruction;
   world-destruction
modality of existence 6n
Mollenhauer, K. 61, 87–8
MOOCs (Massive Open Online Courses) 41
moral education: direct 18
moral reasoning 87
morality 17, 50–1
mortality 10
myth of pedagogy 69

Nazism 61; see also Hitlerism
negative language 19
Nelson, T. 25
neo-liberalism 98; see also freedom
neo-Marxism 5, 61, 80n, 96; see also
   Marxism

Taylor & Francis eBooks

Helping you to choose the right eBooks for your Library

Add Routledge titles to your library's digital collection today. Taylor and Francis ebooks contains over 50,000 titles in the Humanities, Social Sciences, Behavioural Sciences, Built Environment and Law.

Choose from a range of subject packages or create your own!

Benefits for you

» Free MARC records
» COUNTER-compliant usage statistics
» Flexible purchase and pricing options
» All titles DRM-free.

Benefits for your user

» Off-site, anytime access via Athens or referring URL
» Print or copy pages or chapters
» Full content search
» Bookmark, highlight and annotate text
» Access to thousands of pages of quality research at the click of a button.

REQUEST YOUR **FREE** INSTITUTIONAL TRIAL TODAY	**Free Trials Available** We offer free trials to qualifying academic, corporate and government customers.

eCollections – Choose from over 30 subject eCollections, including:

Archaeology	Language Learning
Architecture	Law
Asian Studies	Literature
Business & Management	Media & Communication
Classical Studies	Middle East Studies
Construction	Music
Creative & Media Arts	Philosophy
Criminology & Criminal Justice	Planning
Economics	Politics
Education	Psychology & Mental Health
Energy	Religion
Engineering	Security
English Language & Linguistics	Social Work
Environment & Sustainability	Sociology
Geography	Sport
Health Studies	Theatre & Performance
History	Tourism, Hospitality & Events

For more information, pricing enquiries or to order a free trial, please contact your local sales team: www.tandfebooks.com/page/sales

 Routledge Taylor & Francis Group | The home of Routledge books | **www.tandfebooks.com**